How to Survive As a Woman

Also from EATMS Productions

Books on power, survival, women's autonomy, and the systems shaping modern America.

Nonfiction

Billionaires, Capitalism, and Power

Evil and the Mountain Ungreed
Self Help for American Billionaires
Selfish Steve and the Ivory Tower
Tariffs, Taxes, & Face-Eating Leopards
Ban Billionaires: Fascism Fix

Fascism, Religion, and Cultural Control

Self Help for the Manosphere
Fascism 2025
Fascism & the Perverts & the Greed Virus
Christian Fascism Marriage Book
Tyranny, Table Manners, & Tiramisu

Guides for Women's Autonomy and Protection

How to Survive in Post-America as a Woman
Project 2025 American Drag
4B – Burn, Ban, Boycott, Build
4B OG – So No Go GYN
I'm Glad He's Dead

Analysis of Authoritarian Project 2025

Project 2025: The Blueprint
Project 2025: The List
Project 2025, Christian Dumb Dumbs, & The Republican Agenda
Fascism, Project 2025, & The Pinkprint

Modern Rewrites for Women

Stoic Principles Reimagined
Siddhartha Reimagined
The Prince Reimagined for Women
The Art of War Reimagined for Women
The Jungle Reimagined
The Constitution Reimagined for Women

Machine Learning Series

AI, Bitcoin, Nostr for Women
AI, Safety, & Security for Women
AI, Anxiety, & Health for Women
AI, Kids, & Family Safety for Women
AI, Creativity, & Personal Expression for Women
AI, Independent Work, & Parallel Power for Women

Social Systems Series

Emotional Labor for Women
Household Power for Women
Workplace Power for Women
Medical Bias for Women
Aging Systems for Women
Recovery Systems for Women

Fiction

Dystopian Stories of Resistance and Collapse

Propaganda Paige & the Missing Prosperity
Propaganda Paige & the TIDE Manifesto
Propaganda Paige & the Shadow Cartographers
Propaganda Paige & the Prosperity Alliance
Propaganda Paige & the Shattered Truth
Propaganda Paige & the Rising TIDE
Propaganda Paige & the Last Bastion
Propaganda Paige & the Dawn of Prosperity
Project 2025: Dorian — The Last Men
Project 2025: Boy — A Last Men Novel

How to Survive As a Woman In Post America

Project 2025

How to in Post America 1

by
Esme Mees
& Alice Horton

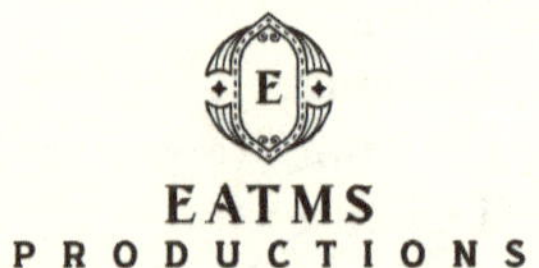

This title is part of an ongoing body of work. All EATMS Productions titles, across all series, authors, and formats, are components of a single connected project.

This book is a work of opinion and creative interpretation. While some names and events may be referenced or alluded to, any claims made are based on publicly available information and are intended as satire, parody, or commentary on societal and political issues. The content should not be interpreted as factual assertions about any individual or entity. The author does not intend to defraud, defame, or mislead, and encourages readers to form their own conclusions. Any resemblance to real persons, living or dead, is purely coincidental unless explicitly noted otherwise.

ISBN: 978-1-966014-06-5

Cover, interior design, interior prints by: Esme Mees

eatms@pm.me
www.eatms.me

Printed in the United States of America.

A strong woman is a woman determined to do something others are determined not be done.

— Marge Piercy

Table of Contents

Introduction
So, This is How it Ends

So, this is how it ends, not with the distant dread we've rehearsed in our imaginations, but with the rude and immediate slap of reality. Project 2025 has dragged us into the Mad Max timeline with all the tact of a wrecking ball, shattering the fragile systems that once kept some semblance of decency intact. The dystopia isn't in some far-off future; it's here, and it's dripping with the oily smugness of men who mistake domination for governance. The Reek regime, with its smarmy overlords and their corporate backers, has taken the blueprint for authoritarianism and sketched their names in every margin. It's not enough for them to win; they need you to lose, and lose completely. They want your autonomy, your dignity, your hope, all of it traded in for a system that rewards the few and grinds the rest into silence.

Let's not mince words: women, children, and families are their first targets. Why? Because compassion, in their eyes, is weakness, and the work of caregiving, be it for a child, an elder, or a struggling community, is a labor they neither understand nor value. Families, especially those led by women, embody a kind of quiet resilience that terrifies men who see control as their birthright. A woman who raises a child on her own terms, who shapes a future that doesn't require permission from the patriarchy, is a threat they cannot abide. So they come for her body first. They dress their intentions in the language of morality and faith, but their actions speak louder: stripping away reproductive rights, criminalizing miscarriages, and blaming her for the consequences of the system they've broken. And when they've wrung her dry, they move on to her children, her neighbors, her community. It's systemic cruelty disguised as governance, and it's as predictable as it is infuriating.

But before we spiral into despair, let's be clear: this manual isn't a eulogy. It's a survival guide, a playbook for resistance, and, perhaps most importantly, a reminder that humanity thrives in defiance of cruelty. Yes, the Reek regime has power, but power is not the same as invincibility. They rely on your compliance, your exhaustion, your belief that nothing can change. They want you to feel small, alone, and incapable. Our first act of resistance is rejecting that lie.

To understand how we've arrived here, we need to dissect the anatomy of their cruelty. Project 2025 is a patchwork of regressive ideologies dressed up as policy, a Frankenstein's monster stitched together from the worst impulses of unchecked capitalism, religious fundamentalism, and good old-fashioned misogyny. It's not subtle. It was never meant to be. Instead, it thrives on overwhelming you, on presenting its horrors so quickly and in such volume that you can't focus on fighting any single part of it. One moment they're gutting healthcare; the next, they're privatizing education. Blink, and they're rewriting environmental protections to serve oil executives. It's deliberate chaos, a strategy borrowed straight from authoritarian regimes the world over: keep the opposition too scattered to organize.

Their cruelty is particularly refined when it comes to women. It's not just about denying us rights, it's about reducing us to roles they can control. In the world of Project 2025, a woman is a womb first, a worker second, and a person never. They'll couch it in terms of protecting "traditional values," but what they really mean is stripping you of autonomy. Want to decide when and if you'll have children? Too bad; your body belongs to the state now. Need access to birth control to manage your health? Suffer a miscarriage? Better hope you can prove it wasn't your fault, or you'll be facing criminal charges. It's a level of control so invasive it would be laughable if it weren't so devastating.

And yet, amidst all this, there is still room for defiance. There is power in naming what they fear most: that we will not comply. That we will not go quietly into the oppressive future they've planned for us. The Reek regime thrives on division, on making you feel isolated in your struggle, but the truth is, you are not alone. For every policy they pass, there are millions who see through it. For every right they strip away, there are countless voices ready to resist. Our strength lies in our ability to connect, to form networks of solidarity that cannot be dismantled by their laws or silenced by their propaganda.

Solidarity, however, is not just a buzzword; it's a practice, and it starts with understanding that survival is not a solo endeavor. The world they're building is designed to pit us against each other, women against men, parents against teachers, workers against one another. Divide and conquer is their oldest trick, and it works only if we let it. To resist, we must see past their divisions and recognize our shared humanity. The single mother trying to keep food on the table, the immigrant family fighting to stay together, the queer couple demanding recognition, they are not just victims of the system; they are allies in the fight to dismantle it.

There is also power in humor, in the act of laughing at their absurdity even as we work to tear it down. Because let's face it, these men are ridiculous. They are terrified of tampons, pronouns, and anything else that reminds them they are not the center of the universe. Their insecurities are the foundation of their cruelty, and exposing that is an act of rebellion. Laugh at their fear of equality, their need to control what they cannot understand, their laughably fragile egos. They want to be seen as gods, untouchable and eternal, but they're just scared little boys in bad suits, playing at power while the world burns around them.

But laughter alone is not enough. Survival in this timeline demands preparation. It means knowing your rights, or what's left of them, and arming yourself with knowledge. It means building community networks that can step in when the systems fail you, because fail you they will. It means learning to navigate a world where your body is a battleground, your choices are policed, and your safety is never guaranteed. And it means recognizing that survival is not the end goal; it's the starting point. To endure is necessary, but to thrive is revolutionary.

As we navigate this Mad Max hellscape, let us remember that dystopias are not eternal. They are constructed, and what is constructed can be dismantled. The Reek regime's power is real, but it is not absolute. It relies on fear, division, and apathy. By rejecting those tools, we begin to reclaim our agency. By standing together, we begin to build something new. And by laughing in their faces, we remind them that no amount of power can erase our humanity.

This is how it ends, yes, but only if we let it. If we choose resistance, choose solidarity, and choose to believe in the possibility of something better, then this isn't the end at all. It's the beginning of a fight they never saw coming. And oh, what a fight it will be.

It's important to understand that survival in this Mad Max timeline isn't just about enduring, it's about building a resistance, both internally and externally. The Reek regime thrives on your exhaustion, your despair, your willingness to accept that this is simply the way things are now. But survival, true survival, is a radical act of defiance. It's about refusing to let them write the ending to this story. It's about finding the cracks in their carefully constructed facade of power and exploiting them with all the creativity, ingenuity, and sheer audacity that they've underestimated. If we are going to survive, we must do more than simply keep our heads above water. We must fight to take back the land, the rights, and the dignity they are so desperate to strip from us.

Resistance begins with rejecting their narratives. They'll tell you this was inevitable, that the fall of rights and freedoms was the natural consequence of some grand moral reckoning. They'll paint themselves as saviors, men (always men) who've restored order to a chaotic world, who've bravely stood up to decadence, and who've saved the nation from itself. This is, of course, a lie. There is no moral high ground in a system that punishes women for having miscarriages, that criminalizes poverty, and that strips families of the basic resources they need to survive. There is no salvation in policies that hand the earth's future to oil barons while calling birth control a pollutant. They'll wrap their tyranny in the flag, in scripture, in whatever symbols they think will make their cruelty more palatable. But a gilded cage is still a cage. And their entire regime is built on convincing you to decorate your own chains.

So how do you resist when every lever of power has been co-opted by people who despise you? First, you must build your own power. That starts with community. The Reek regime is terrified of connection because it knows that solidarity is its kryptonite. Their policies are designed to isolate you, to make you think that your struggle is unique, your burden yours alone to bear. But this is another lie. If they're coming for your reproductive rights, your neighbor's healthcare, and your coworker's housing, then your fight is their fight, too. Find your people. Build networks of mutual aid and support. The government may have dismantled the safety nets, but we can create our own, woven together with trust and shared purpose. These networks don't have to be grand or revolutionary in appearance to be effective. Sometimes resistance looks like pooling resources with your community so no one goes hungry. Sometimes it's creating childcare co-ops when affordable daycare has been gutted. Sometimes it's sharing information about underground clinics, alternative schools, or safe routes for those needing to flee abusive systems. Small acts of defiance add up. They create the infrastructure for larger movements, and they remind us that even when the system fails, we still have each other.

But community alone isn't enough. Resistance also requires courage. It requires speaking out when staying silent feels safer. It requires standing up when sitting down feels like the more comfortable option. The Reek regime wants you to believe that their power is absolute, that fighting back is futile. This, like everything else they say, is a lie. Power is only as strong as the fear it generates, and fear is a fragile thing. It cracks under the weight of a single brave voice, one that says, "No. Not today." Courage is contagious. When you speak out, you give others permission to do the same. When you stand up, you remind them that they can, too. And when enough of us stand together, even the mightiest regimes begin to falter.

Of course, courage isn't just about bold acts of public defiance. Sometimes it's about doing the quiet, unglamorous work that sustains a movement. It's about listening to your neighbor's fears and saying, "I'm here for you." It's about organizing supply chains for protestors or opening your home to someone in need. It's about refusing to look away when the world tells you to mind your own business. Courage is showing up, day after day, even when the victories are small, even when the setbacks feel crushing. It's planting seeds in the middle of a storm, trusting that one day, something beautiful will grow.

As we resist, we must also prepare. This is not a fight that will be won quickly, nor is it one that can be waged without strategy. Preparation means understanding the systems you're up against. It means knowing your rights, or what's left of them, and learning how to protect yourself when those rights are violated. It means being ready to document abuses, to share stories, to hold the powerful accountable even when they think no one is watching. Preparation also means taking care of yourself and those around you. Burnout is real, and it's a tool of the oppressor. They want you to exhaust yourself, to feel like your efforts are futile. Rest is resistance. Joy is resistance. Find the things that keep your fire burning and guard them fiercely.

And let's not forget humor. Oh, how they hate to be laughed at. The Reek regime takes itself so seriously, painting its leaders as saviors, its policies as divine mandates. But peel back the layers, and you'll find a group of men who are utterly terrified, terrified of change, of equality, of losing the power they've hoarded for so long. They are scared little boys in big suits, wielding cruelty because it's the only tool they've ever known. Laugh at them. Mock their absurdities. Point out the contradictions in their rhetoric, the hypocrisies in their actions. Humor doesn't just diffuse fear; it exposes their weaknesses. And a regime exposed is a regime that can be toppled.

But survival in this timeline isn't just about defying the Reek regime; it's about imagining a world beyond it. It's about refusing to accept that this is all there is, that their vision of society is the only one possible. Dystopias are not inevitable. They are constructed by the choices of those in power. And what is constructed can be dismantled. Even as we resist, we must dream. We must imagine a future where our bodies are our own, where our communities are strong, and where justice is not a privilege but a right. We must hold onto these dreams, not as distant fantasies but as blueprints for the world we are fighting to create.

This is not the end. It feels like it, perhaps, standing here in the rubble of what we once called progress. But history has shown us time and time again that darkness does not last forever. Empires fall. Regimes crumble. Oppressors are overthrown. What determines the future is not the strength of their power but the resilience of our hope. They can take many things from us, our rights, our resources, even our lives, but they cannot take our capacity to hope, to fight, to believe in something better. That is ours, and it always will be.

So, here we are, at the beginning of what feels like the end. It's terrifying, yes, but it's also an opportunity, a chance to rewrite the story, to reclaim the narrative, to build a world that is kinder, fairer, and more just than anything the Reek regime could ever imagine. Let them think they've won. Let them bask in the fleeting glow of their power. We know better. We know that power built on fear is power that cannot last. And we are ready to outlast them. Together, we will survive. Together, we will resist. And together, we will rise.

Top Things to Do Now to Prepare

Start Building Community Connections

Find local groups focused on mutual aid, reproductive justice, or activism. Attend meetings, volunteer, and connect with people who share your values. A strong community will be vital for emotional support, resource sharing, and organized resistance.

Create an Emergency Fund

Begin saving money specifically for emergencies related to reproductive healthcare or other urgent needs. Even small contributions add up and can make a significant difference in a crisis.

Learn Basic Legal Rights and Resources

Understand what reproductive rights exist in your state and how they're enforced. Identify local and national organizations offering legal aid or advocacy, and keep their contact information handy.

Get Informed About Underground Networks

Familiarize yourself with trusted organizations or informal networks that provide access to reproductive healthcare, contraception, or abortion support. Research how to safely connect with these resources if needed.

Secure Your Personal Documents and Plans

Keep important documents- ID, medical records, prescriptions, and emergency contacts, in a secure, accessible place. Create a backup plan for situations where you may need to travel for care or assistance. Clear, prepared steps can reduce stress in emergencies.

Practice Digital Security

Use encrypted messaging apps like Signal for sensitive conversations. Avoid discussing reproductive health issues on social media or insecure platforms. Secure your devices with strong passwords and enable two-factor authentication.

Cultivate Joy and Rest

This is a long fight, and burnout is a real risk. Make space for joy, laughter, and moments of peace. Rest isn't just self-care, it's a revolutionary act in a world that wants you exhausted

The Ten Plagues of Project 2025
1~The War on Wombs

The War on Wombs is not a new chapter in history but an all-too-familiar one rewritten with brutal efficiency under Project 2025. Women's bodies have always been battlegrounds, contested spaces where power and control collide. But now, the war has reached an apex, waged openly and unapologetically by a regime determined to dismantle decades of progress. Abortion? Gone. Birth control? Vilified. Miscarriage? Investigated like a crime scene. The Reek regime has taken aim at the most fundamental aspect of bodily autonomy, declaring that your womb is no longer yours. Instead, it is a vessel for their agenda, a symbol of their power, and, if you resist, a weapon they will wield against you.

In this new reality, the first thing you must accept is that your body is under surveillance, not metaphorically, but literally. State governments are rushing to implement technologies and policies designed to track your reproductive status. Period-tracking apps, once harmless tools for managing cycles, have become potential informants. A missed period might not just mean pregnancy; it could mean scrutiny. This is the level of control they seek, where every choice, every action, every natural process of your body becomes data they can weaponize. The message is clear: You are not to be trusted with your own body.

Under Project 2025, the Reek regime has cloaked its war on women in the language of morality and family values. They say they are protecting life, but whose life? It's certainly not the life of the woman forced to carry a pregnancy that threatens her health. It's not the life of the teenager raped by a family member, told by the state that she must bear her abuser's child. It's not the life of the single mother struggling to provide for the children she already has. No, the lives they protect are abstract, theoretical, a means to justify their control. Once that life is born, it is discarded, left to fend for itself in a world stripped of safety nets and support systems. This isn't about life. It's about domination.

If you're not allowed to choose whether to carry a pregnancy, your only recourse becomes navigating the treacherous world of black-market care. Let's be honest: This isn't the first time women have been forced into the shadows to exercise control over their bodies. History is rife with stories of women helping each other in secret, creating networks of care where none officially existed. And while it's infuriating that we must once again resort to these measures, it's also a testament to our resilience. When systems fail, we build our own.

Underground networks are already forming, a patchwork quilt of solidarity spanning cities, states, and borders. These networks are lifelines, connecting those in need with those willing to help. They are the modern Underground Railroad, complete with safe houses, trusted contacts, and encrypted communications. If you find yourself in need of these services, know that you are not alone. But also know that the risks are real. The Reek regime will stop at nothing to dismantle these networks, to punish those who dare to help, to make examples of those who resist. This is why discretion is critical. Choose your allies carefully. Verify your sources. And above all, trust your instincts.

Black-market care extends beyond abortion. Birth control, once as simple as a trip to the pharmacy, has become a controlled substance in many states. The Reek regime has spun a narrative that birth control is poisoning the environment, that it's an affront to God's design, that it's unnecessary for women who should be focused on motherhood. These arguments are as absurd as they are dangerous. Birth control is not just a tool for family planning; it's a cornerstone of women's health. It treats conditions like endometriosis and polycystic ovary syndrome. It allows women to work, to study, to live their lives on their own terms. Denying access to birth control is denying women the right to exist as full and autonomous beings.

So, what do you do when the pharmacy shelves are bare, and the doctor's office is closed to you? You turn to alternatives. The same networks that provide access to abortion services are also working to distribute contraception. Emergency contraceptives like Plan B, long-lasting options like IUDs, and even birth control pills are being stockpiled and shared discreetly. Online communities are stepping up, offering advice on where to find supplies and how to use them safely. But with every workaround comes a risk. Buying medication online can be dangerous if you're not careful. Counterfeit products, unreliable dosages, and legal repercussions are all possibilities. This is the reality of a world where your rights have been legislated out of existence.

The criminalization of miscarriage is perhaps the most chilling aspect of this war on wombs. Imagine losing a pregnancy, a loss already fraught with grief and pain, only to find yourself accused of causing it. Did you drink too much coffee? Did you lift something heavy? Did you fail to follow the state's prescribed guidelines for proper behavior during pregnancy? These questions are not hypothetical. Women are already being prosecuted for miscarriages, their tragedies treated as crimes. The burden of proof falls on the accused, forcing them to defend their innocence in a system designed to presume their guilt. This is not justice; it's an inquisition.

In this dystopian landscape, survival requires vigilance and resourcefulness. Educate yourself about your options. Learn how to navigate the underground networks, how to access the care you need without drawing attention. Connect with others who share your plight, because there is strength in numbers. And don't let them rob you of your humanity. They may treat you as a vessel, a statistic, a pawn in their game, but you are so much more than that. You are a person with dreams, desires, and the right to live a life of your own choosing. The war on wombs is brutal, but it is not insurmountable. Women have faced these battles before and emerged stronger, more united, more determined. This is not the end of the story. It's a chapter, and like all chapters, it will eventually close. What comes next is up to us. Will we allow their narrative to stand, or will we write our own? The answer lies in our hands, and in the hands of those who refuse to let this war define us.

The War on Wombs is not just about policy, it's a full-scale assault on autonomy, identity, and humanity. Under Project 2025, the regime has not only declared your body a battleground but has also constructed a labyrinth of barriers to trap you. If the first salvo was stripping away access to abortion and birth control, the second is ensuring that even attempting to navigate their system is an act of desperation. The Reek regime thrives on creating an environment so hostile, so demoralizing, that you begin to believe their narrative: that you're powerless, that you're alone, that the fight isn't worth it. But here's the truth, they are terrified of your resistance. Every oppressive law they pass is an admission of their fear. They know that control is fleeting, and they will do anything to keep it, no matter the cost.

The regime's war strategy relies heavily on misinformation. Their propaganda machine churns out narratives designed to confuse, divide, and demoralize. Abortion becomes "murder," birth control becomes "poison," and women seeking autonomy are labeled as selfish, immoral, or worse. These lies seep into every corner of public discourse, creating a culture where shame and stigma are tools of enforcement. It's not enough for them to pass laws; they need society itself to act as an accomplice. Your neighbors, coworkers, and even family members are encouraged to police your behavior, report your choices, and enforce their version of morality. This decentralized surveillance system ensures that the war on wombs isn't just waged in courts and legislatures, it's waged in your home, your workplace, and your community.

Navigating this landscape requires a dual strategy: resistance and resilience. Resistance means refusing to internalize their narratives. You are not selfish for wanting control over your own body. You are not immoral for seeking to avoid or terminate a pregnancy. These are lies meant to shame you into submission. Recognize them for what they are: weapons wielded by a regime that fears your autonomy. Resilience, on the other hand, is about maintaining your strength in the face of constant attack. It's about finding ways to care for yourself and your community, even when the world feels like it's falling apart.

One of the first steps in resilience is understanding the underground networks that have formed in response to this crisis. These networks are lifelines, but they require careful navigation. The people involved are risking everything to help others, privacy, safety, even their freedom. Whether it's accessing abortion pills, finding a provider willing to defy state laws, or obtaining birth control, these networks operate on trust. They thrive on discretion and mutual aid. To engage with these networks, you must be both cautious and courageous. Vet your sources carefully. Seek recommendations from trusted allies. Use encrypted communications whenever possible. And remember, while the stakes are high for everyone involved, they are often highest for the most vulnerable, those with the least access to resources, those living under the harshest laws, and those already marginalized by society.

While these networks are crucial, they are not a sustainable solution. They are stopgaps in a system that has failed spectacularly. The long-term fight must involve dismantling the very structures that made these networks necessary. This is not just about regaining what has been lost, it's about building something better. The Reek regime's policies are not an anomaly; they are the result of a system that has always prioritized control over compassion, profit over people. If we are to truly end this war, we must address the root causes of oppression. That means fighting not just for reproductive rights but for economic justice, racial equity, and universal access to healthcare. These battles are interconnected. Victory in one arena strengthens the fight in another.

At the same time, we must acknowledge the toll this fight takes on individuals, particularly those on the frontlines. Activists, providers, and those directly impacted by these policies face immense pressure. Burnout is real, and it is a tool of the oppressor. The Reek regime hopes you'll exhaust yourself, that you'll give up out of sheer fatigue. This is why self-care is not a luxury, it is a necessity. Rest is resistance. Joy is resistance. Finding moments of happiness, connection, and love in the midst of chaos is an act of defiance. Take care of yourself not just because you deserve it, but because the fight needs you at your strongest.

It's also essential to recognize that the war on wombs doesn't affect all women equally. Wealthy women will always find ways to access care, even if it means traveling across state or national borders. The burden of these policies falls disproportionately on those who are already marginalized, low-income women, women of color, undocumented women, and trans and nonbinary individuals who need reproductive healthcare. This is by design. The Reek regime uses these policies as tools of oppression, reinforcing existing hierarchies and deepening systemic inequalities. To fight this war effectively, we must center the voices and experiences of those most impacted. Their stories are not just heartbreaking, they are galvanizing. They reveal the true cost of these policies and the urgent need for change.

One of the most insidious aspects of the war on wombs is the criminalization of reproductive healthcare. Women are being prosecuted for miscarriages, accused of endangering their pregnancies through perfectly normal behavior. Doctors are being forced to choose between following their oath to do no harm and obeying laws that threaten their livelihoods. Pharmacists are refusing to fill prescriptions for medications that could potentially be used to induce abortion. This culture of fear and criminalization doesn't just hurt individuals, it erodes trust in the entire healthcare system. Women are less likely to seek care if they believe they'll be judged, investigated, or punished. This creates a ripple effect, where preventable complications become life-threatening emergencies, and healthcare providers are driven out of practice.

In this climate, educating yourself about your options is critical. Know your rights, even as they are being stripped away. Learn the laws in your state, but also understand that these laws are not absolute. There are ways to navigate around them, ways to access the care you need without exposing yourself to unnecessary risk. Resources like abortion funds, legal aid organizations, and advocacy groups are working tirelessly to provide information and support. Familiarize yourself with their work and don't hesitate to reach out when you need help. And if you are in a position to do so, consider supporting these organizations. Their work is essential, and they cannot do it alone.

At its core, the war on wombs is about control, who has it, who doesn't, and who decides. The Reek regime's policies are an attempt to assert control over the most intimate aspects of our lives, to dictate not only what we can do with our bodies but who we are allowed to be. But control is not the same as power. True power lies in the ability to shape your own destiny, to make choices based on your values and your needs. This is what they fear most, your power, your autonomy, your humanity. They can pass laws, spread lies, and punish dissent, but they cannot take away your ability to resist. That is yours, and it is stronger than they will ever understand.

The war on wombs is brutal, and the path ahead is daunting. But history has shown us that oppression is not invincible. It can be challenged, disrupted, and ultimately defeated. Women have been fighting these battles for centuries, and we have always found ways to endure, to resist, and to rise. This moment is no different. It is our turn to take up the fight, to refuse to be silenced, and to demand a better future, not just for ourselves but for everyone who comes after us. Because the war on wombs is not just about women, it's about humanity. And humanity, when it refuses to bow to cruelty, is unstoppable.

The war on wombs does not end with the dismantling of rights or the criminalization of autonomy, it extends into a chilling, calculated cultural shift that seeks to normalize these attacks. This is the third, most insidious front of the battle: the reshaping of societal values to align with the Reek regime's agenda. The ultimate goal isn't just to control the laws; it's to control the narrative, to make the subjugation of women seem inevitable, natural, even righteous. This is not just policy, it's propaganda, aimed at breaking not just your body but your spirit. Yet, even in this calculated assault, there is opportunity. Because for all their efforts, they cannot erase the truth: that resistance is woven into the fabric of humanity, that even in the darkest times, people fight back.

This cultural war is fought on multiple fronts. In schools, curriculums are rewritten to erase the history of reproductive rights, turning decades of struggle into footnotes or outright omissions. In media, stories of women's autonomy are reframed as cautionary tales, while those who conform to the regime's vision of womanhood are lauded as paragons of virtue. Even in the public square, art, literature, and conversation are co-opted to reinforce the idea that a woman's worth is measured solely by her reproductive capabilities. This is a regime that seeks to rewrite the very essence of identity, reducing women to symbols of their control.

And yet, culture is a fickle thing, far harder to control than legislation. While the Reek regime pours its resources into propaganda, resistance takes root in the cracks they cannot see. Underground networks don't just provide access to healthcare, they share stories, art, and ideas that challenge the regime's narrative. Protest signs become symbols of defiance, books are smuggled like contraband, and whispered conversations in classrooms plant seeds of doubt in the minds of a generation they thought they could mold. Culture, like nature, has a way of growing back, no matter how often it is cut down.

One of the most potent tools of cultural resistance is storytelling. The regime thrives on silencing dissent, but every story shared is a spark that refuses to go out. Stories of those who fought for their autonomy, of those who found ways to care for others despite the odds, of those who refused to comply even when compliance seemed inevitable, these stories are weapons in the war for truth. They remind us that we are not alone, that our struggles are shared, and that resistance is not just possible but necessary. Storytelling is more than catharsis; it is a way to reclaim agency, to say, "This is who I am, and you cannot take that from me."

Education, too, becomes a battlefield. In a world where schools are forced to conform to the regime's narrative, teaching the truth becomes an act of rebellion. Parents, teachers, and students form quiet alliances, sharing knowledge that isn't in the textbooks, questioning the narratives presented in classrooms. Libraries, both physical and digital, become sanctuaries of forbidden knowledge. The regime may try to control the curriculum, but they cannot control curiosity, and curiosity is the first step toward defiance. Art and creativity flourish in resistance. Music, poetry, and visual art become expressions of defiance, channels for emotions that cannot be silenced. A mural painted in the dead of night, a song shared anonymously online, a poem whispered in a gathering, all of these are acts of rebellion that cannot be legislated away. Art transcends the barriers they build, speaking to the humanity they try so hard to suppress. It is a reminder that while they may hold power, they do not hold the soul of a people.

The war on wombs is brutal and pervasive, but it is not without hope. Hope lies in the connections we build, the stories we share, the knowledge we pass down, and the art we create. It lies in our ability to see through their lies, to resist their narratives, and to imagine a future that looks nothing like the one they have planned. It lies in every act of defiance, no matter how small, and in the recognition that survival is itself a victory. The regime seeks to write us out of history, but we are not so easily erased. We are here, we are fighting, and we are building a future that they cannot imagine. Let them come for our rights, our bodies, our stories. We will not bow. We will not break. We will survive. This war will end, and when it does, it will be our voices, our art, and our resilience that echo through history, long after their power has crumbled to dust.

Checklist to Prepare for the War on Wombs

Delete Period Tracking Apps

Many period-tracking apps collect and share your data with third parties, making them potential tools for surveillance in states with restrictive laws. Switch to tracking your cycle on a physical calendar or use a secure, encrypted method if digital tracking is essential. Prioritize privacy in all health-related data.

Secure Access to Birth Control and Emergency Contraceptives

If you use hormonal birth control or Plan B, consider stocking up now. Talk to your healthcare provider about long-term options like IUDs or implants, which can provide years of contraception without needing frequent access to a pharmacy. Research trusted sources for emergency contraception and know how to obtain them discreetly.

Learn About Reproductive Health Resources

Educate yourself on organizations and networks providing support for reproductive healthcare, including abortion funds, telehealth providers, and mutual aid groups. Familiarize yourself with resources like Aid Access or Plan C Pills, which can guide you on accessing safe care in restrictive areas.

Get Physically Healthy

Prioritize your physical health by maintaining a balanced diet, staying active, and addressing any underlying medical conditions. A healthier body is more resilient to stress and better prepared for the physical demands of navigating difficult circumstances.

Focus on Mental Health

The fight ahead will be emotionally taxing. Consider therapy or counseling if it's available to you, and develop coping strategies like mindfulness, journaling, or connecting with loved ones. Build habits that support your mental resilience, such as setting boundaries and prioritizing rest.

The Ten Plagues of Project 2025
2~Welcome to Healthcare Hell

Welcome to Healthcare Hell, where compassion is a liability, affordability is a pipe dream, and accessibility depends entirely on your zip code and income bracket. Under Project 2025, the healthcare system has been systematically dismantled, repackaged, and sold off to the highest bidder, leaving millions stranded without care. The promise of "freedom" from government interference has resulted in a nightmare of corporate control, where profits dictate policy and human lives are just numbers on a spreadsheet. Maternal mortality rates are soaring, life-saving procedures are delayed or denied, and the act of seeking care has become an act of bravery. The Reek regime's healthcare overhaul wasn't a mistake, it was a calculated move. By gutting protections, repealing laws like the Affordable Care Act, and privatizing as many systems as possible, they ensured that only the wealthiest have access to comprehensive care. For everyone else, healthcare is now a luxury, not a right. If you're pregnant, if you're chronically ill, if you're aging, or even if you're just unlucky enough to get hurt, you're caught in a system designed to extract every penny you have before spitting you out, worse off than when you started.

Let's begin with maternal healthcare, or what's left of it. Maternal mortality rates, already higher in the United States than in most developed nations, have spiked dramatically. Hospitals in rural and underserved areas are closing their maternity wards, leaving entire regions without obstetric care. Women are forced to drive hundreds of miles for prenatal appointments or risk delivering in emergency rooms ill-equipped for childbirth. For Black women and other women of color, the statistics are even grimmer. Racial disparities in maternal care, long ignored, are now exacerbated by policies that actively undermine public health. Miscarriages, once regarded as tragic but natural occurrences, have become criminalized. Under the Reek regime's anti-abortion policies, every pregnancy loss is viewed with suspicion. Did you eat the wrong foods? Drink a glass of wine before you knew you were pregnant? Skip a doctor's appointment because you couldn't afford it? These questions aren't hypothetical; they're part of a growing wave of investigations and prosecutions aimed at women who miscarry. The burden of proof falls on you to show that your loss was "natural," a nearly impossible task in a system that presumes guilt. This isn't just a war on reproductive rights; it's a war on women's humanity.

Chronic illness is another casualty of the healthcare crisis. Medications for conditions like diabetes, asthma, and heart disease have become prohibitively expensive, as pharmaceutical companies capitalize on the lack of regulation. Insulin, a drug that's been around for over a century, is now priced out of reach for many, leading to rationing and preventable deaths. Meanwhile, preventative care has all but disappeared for those without comprehensive insurance, creating a cascade of medical emergencies that could have been avoided. It's a vicious cycle: the less care you receive, the sicker you become, and the more expensive your treatment grows, if you can afford it at all.

Mental health, already a neglected area of care, has been pushed even further to the margins. Funding for mental health programs has been slashed, leaving those struggling with anxiety, depression, PTSD, and other conditions with few options. Suicide rates are climbing, particularly among young people and marginalized groups, while access to therapy and psychiatric care dwindles. The stigma surrounding mental illness, amplified by a regime that equates vulnerability with weakness, prevents many from seeking help until it's too late.

If this sounds bleak, that's because it is. But even in the face of this hellscape, there are ways to protect yourself and your loved ones. Survival in this system requires a combination of knowledge, preparation, and, whenever possible, collective action. Start by understanding the resources available in your area. Federally Qualified Health Centers (FQHCs) still provide care on a sliding scale, though they're under immense strain. Nonprofit organizations, free clinics, and community health programs can fill some gaps, though they, too, are overwhelmed. Know where these services are located, what they offer, and how to access them before you're in crisis. For those with chronic illnesses, preparation is critical. Stockpile medications when you can, but be mindful of expiration dates and storage requirements. Explore patient assistance programs offered by pharmaceutical companies, though imperfect, they can provide temporary relief. Learn about alternative treatments and therapies, but be cautious of unproven or unsafe options marketed as quick fixes. Your health is too important to gamble with, no matter how desperate the situation.

In addition to physical health, prioritize your mental well-being. Build a support network of friends, family, or community groups who can help you navigate the emotional toll of living in a broken system. Practice self-care, whether through mindfulness, exercise, or creative outlets that bring you joy. And don't underestimate the power of collective advocacy. Join organizations fighting for healthcare reform, and use your voice to demand change. The Reek regime wants you to believe that resistance is futile, but history shows us that collective action can topple even the most entrenched systems.

Healthcare Hell isn't just about the system itself, it's about the culture of fear and control that underpins it. The Reek regime has weaponized healthcare to enforce compliance and punish dissent. If you step out of line, by seeking an abortion, by protesting their policies, by simply existing as a marginalized person, you risk losing access to the care you need to survive. This is healthcare as a tool of oppression, where the goal is not to heal but to control. And yet, even in the face of this, people find ways to resist. Communities come together to support one another, activists fight tirelessly for change, and individuals refuse to let the regime define their worth.

As we navigate this new reality, it's essential to remember that healthcare is not a privilege, it's a human right. The Reek regime's policies are a direct assault on that principle, but they cannot erase the truth. Every act of defiance, every effort to care for yourself and others, is a step toward reclaiming that right. It won't be easy, and it won't be quick, but the fight for healthcare justice is a fight worth waging. After all, the alternative is not just unacceptable, it's unthinkable.

The second part of *Welcome to* Healthcare Hell delves deeper into the fractures in the system under Project 2025, where survival is increasingly a matter of luck, privilege, and sheer willpower. As the regime's policies solidify, the chasm between those who can access care and those who cannot widens, leaving millions to fend for themselves in a system designed to discard the most vulnerable. The question isn't just how we survive in this dystopian healthcare landscape, it's how we fight back and build something better.

One of the starkest consequences of Project 2025's healthcare dismantling is the evaporation of safety nets. Medicaid, once a lifeline for low-income families, has been gutted to the point of irrelevance. Those who relied on it for basic care, children, pregnant women, people with disabilities, are now left to navigate a system where their existence is considered a burden. Emergency rooms, once the last resort for those without insurance, are overwhelmed, turning away patients who don't meet their ever-narrowing criteria for care. The concept of triage has been corrupted, not by medical necessity but by economic gatekeeping. If you can't pay, you're expendable.

This erosion of safety nets has cascading effects on families. Parents are forced to make impossible choices between paying for a child's medication or putting food on the table. Routine illnesses spiral into life-threatening conditions because the cost of a doctor's visit is too high. Preventable deaths become commonplace, not because the solutions don't exist, but because they've been priced out of reach. This is healthcare in the Reek regime's America: a cruel game of survival where the odds are stacked against you unless you're rich.

The impact on reproductive healthcare remains devastating. Maternity care has become a privilege for the few, with out-of-pocket costs skyrocketing and coverage for prenatal services disappearing under many insurance plans. Home births and midwifery, once empowering alternatives, are now fraught with legal and logistical hurdles, as the regime seeks to control not just if you give birth but how and where. The rise in maternal mortality is not an accident, it's a predictable result of policies that prioritize control over care.

Black women, already disproportionately affected by healthcare disparities, are dying at even higher rates, victims of a system that sees their lives as expendable. For those seeking abortion care, the landscape is even more perilous. With bans in place across much of the country, pregnant people are turning to underground networks for help. But these networks, while lifesaving, are under siege. Activists, providers, and even those who simply offer transportation are being prosecuted under harsh new laws. Crossing state lines to access care has become a high-stakes gamble, with surveillance and reporting mechanisms in place to catch those who dare to defy the regime. This criminalization extends beyond abortion to miscarriages, as women are interrogated and investigated for the loss of pregnancies that, under a just system, would be met with compassion and care.

Chronic illness and disability add another layer of vulnerability. For those living with long-term conditions, access to medication, therapies, and specialized care has become a nightmare. The privatization of healthcare has placed lifesaving treatments in the hands of corporations whose sole interest is profit. Drugs like insulin are hoarded, their prices inflated to astronomical levels, while insurance companies deny coverage for treatments deemed "non-essential." For those with disabilities, the rollback of protections under laws like the Americans with Disabilities Act has made an already difficult existence nearly impossible. The message is clear: If you are not "productive" by the regime's standards, your life is not worth preserving.

Mental health care, too, is in crisis. Funding for community mental health programs has been slashed, leaving millions without access to therapy, medication, or crisis intervention. Suicide hotlines are underfunded and understaffed, and inpatient facilities are closing their doors. The stigma surrounding mental illness, fueled by the regime's narrative of self-reliance and moral superiority, prevents many from seeking help. Those who do often face insurmountable barriers, from cost to availability. The result is a silent epidemic, where the pain of millions goes unseen and untreated.

Amid this devastation, communities are finding ways to resist and rebuild. Mutual aid networks are stepping in where the system has failed, providing everything from medication to transportation to emotional support. Grassroots organizations are mobilizing to fight back against regressive policies, using everything from legal challenges to direct action. Healthcare workers, many of whom are themselves victims of this broken system, are forming unions and organizing strikes to demand better conditions for their patients and themselves. These acts of defiance, while often small and localized, are lifelines in a sea of despair.

Technology has also become a double-edged sword in the fight for healthcare justice. On one hand, digital platforms have made it easier to share information, organize protests, and connect people with resources. On the other hand, these same tools are being used by the regime to surveil, track, and prosecute those who defy their laws. Period-tracking apps, online pharmacies, and even social media platforms are being weaponized against the very people they were designed to help. Navigating this digital minefield requires vigilance, encryption, and a healthy dose of skepticism.

While survival is the immediate goal, it is not enough. The fight for healthcare justice must go beyond merely enduring the present crisis. It must be about envisioning and building a system that values every life equally, that prioritizes care over profit, that sees health as a human right rather than a privilege. This vision requires bold action: universal healthcare, the regulation of pharmaceutical and insurance companies, the dismantling of for-profit hospitals, and the expansion of public health initiatives. It requires acknowledging and addressing the systemic inequalities that have always existed in our healthcare system, from racial disparities to geographic barriers. The road ahead is daunting, but it is not hopeless. The Reek regime's policies are unsustainable, built on the exploitation and suffering of the many for the benefit of the few. Resistance, while difficult, is not futile. Every act of defiance, every mutual aid network, every community clinic that opens its doors is a step toward a better future. Healthcare Hell is a reality now, but it doesn't have to be permanent. The fight to reclaim our humanity, our dignity, and our right to live is just beginning. Together, we can turn this hell into something resembling hope.

Checklist to Prepare for Healthcare Hell

Identify Local Healthcare Resources

Research free clinics, community health centers, and nonprofit organizations in your area. Keep a list of their services, locations, and operating hours.

Secure Your Medical Records

Request copies of your medical records and store them in a safe place. Ensure you have digital backups stored securely, preferably encrypted.

Learn Basic First Aid and Emergency Care
Take a first aid and CPR class to prepare for minor emergencies. Create a comprehensive first-aid kit tailored to your family's needs, including supplies for chronic conditions.

Stock Up on Over-the-Counter Medications
Purchase pain relievers, cold medicine, allergy medication, and other essentials. These can become difficult to access in emergencies or high-demand periods.

Find Alternative Healthcare Options
Explore holistic, community-based, or alternative treatments that can supplement traditional care when access is limited. Research reputable providers and organizations offering these services.

Build a Healthcare Support Network
Connect with neighbors, friends, or local groups willing to share resources, transportation, or caregiving in case of medical needs.

Research Telehealth Options
Identify virtual healthcare services that offer consultations, prescriptions, or advice. Many telehealth platforms are more affordable and accessible than in-person visits.

Understand Patient Assistance Programs
Familiarize yourself with pharmaceutical companies' assistance programs for discounted or free medication. Bookmark application sites for easy access.

Learn Self-Advocacy Skills
Practice asking questions, documenting interactions, and advocating for your needs in medical settings. Being prepared to assert your rights can improve outcomes in a fractured system.

Stay Updated on Healthcare Advocacy
Follow advocacy groups and organizations fighting for healthcare reform. Staying informed empowers you to take action and access up-to-date resources.

The Ten Plagues of Project 2025
3~The Corporate Hunger Games

The Corporate Hunger Games have arrived, and unlike the dystopian fiction they seem ripped from, there's no grand arena or lavish Capitol city to marvel at. Instead, it's an endless grind, a day-to-day scramble for survival in a workforce where deregulated industries and gutted labor protections have turned even the most basic jobs into ruthless battles for crumbs. Under Project 2025, the balance of power in the workplace has shifted even further toward employers, leaving workers, particularly women and caregivers, at the mercy of a system designed to exploit, overwork, and underpay them. "Leaning in" has been exposed as a hollow platitude when the ladder you're climbing has been greased by the very companies profiting from your labor. Now, survival means not just navigating this system but finding ways to resist and reclaim your dignity in a world that treats you as disposable.

The first salvo in this new corporate landscape was the systematic dismantling of labor protections. Workers' rights, already precarious, were further eroded as the Reek regime repealed regulations and underfunded enforcement agencies like OSHA and the Department of Labor. Wage theft has become rampant, with employers emboldened by the lack of oversight. Unpaid overtime, denial of benefits, and misclassification of workers as independent contractors are now standard practices in many industries. Companies no longer fear consequences because the system no longer holds them accountable. For those in low-wage and caregiving jobs, sectors dominated by women, particularly women of color, the impact has been devastating. The promise of fair treatment has been replaced by the threat of replacement: if you complain, you're out. If you can't keep up, someone else will take your place.

Caregiving jobs often considered "women's work," have been hit hardest. Nurses, home health aides, childcare providers, these roles, critical to the functioning of society, have been stripped of dignity and fair compensation. The pandemic revealed their importance, yet instead of investing in these workers, the Reek regime has doubled down on exploitation. Many caregivers are now forced to work long hours for poverty wages, without access to healthcare or paid leave. The physical and emotional toll of caregiving is compounded by financial insecurity, leaving workers drained and desperate. For many, the job is no longer about passion or purpose but pure survival.

Deregulation has further emboldened corporations to cut corners, creating dangerous working conditions across industries. Factories, warehouses, and construction sites are operating with minimal safety standards, resulting in preventable injuries and deaths. Women, often relegated to the lowest-paying and least-protected positions, bear the brunt of this negligence. In workplaces where sexual harassment and discrimination were already pervasive, the absence of oversight has turned bad situations into outright hostile environments. Reporting abuse is risky when retaliation is swift and jobs are scarce. The choice is clear: endure the abuse or risk losing your livelihood.

The gig economy, once heralded as a flexible alternative to traditional employment, has been weaponized under Project 2025. Companies like Uber, DoorDash, and Amazon now wield immense power over their workers, who are classified as independent contractors and thus denied basic protections like health insurance, sick leave, and workers' compensation. For women, who often rely on gig work to balance caregiving responsibilities, this lack of security is especially cruel. The illusion of flexibility shatters the moment you realize that an algorithm determines your earnings, your schedule, and your job security. There's no HR department to turn to, no union to advocate for you, and no safety net when things go wrong.

In this cutthroat environment, survival requires a new playbook. The first step is understanding your rights, even as they are being stripped away. While labor protections have been gutted at the federal level, some states and municipalities still enforce stronger worker protections. Knowing where you stand legally can help you advocate for yourself and push back against exploitative practices. Keep records of your hours worked, wages paid, and any incidents of mistreatment. Documentation is your strongest weapon in a dispute, even in a system rigged against you.

Building solidarity with other workers is another crucial survival strategy. The Reek regime's policies are designed to isolate and divide workers, pitting them against one another in a race to the bottom.

Don't fall into the trap of seeing your coworkers as competitors. Instead, foster a sense of community and shared purpose. Organizing efforts may be risky, but they are also essential. Even small acts of solidarity, like sharing information about workplace rights or supporting a colleague facing mistreatment, can make a difference. The corporate machine thrives on fear and division; unity is its greatest threat.

For women in caregiving roles, survival often means seeking out community support networks. Grassroots organizations and mutual aid groups have become lifelines, providing everything from financial assistance to childcare. These networks are not just about meeting immediate needs, they are about building resilience and resistance. By pooling resources and sharing knowledge, caregivers can begin to challenge the systems that exploit them. It's not easy work, but it is necessary.

Another critical element of survival is self-care, though not in the commodified sense often marketed to women. True self-care in this environment means setting boundaries, prioritizing your health, and finding ways to recharge despite the chaos. It means recognizing that burnout is not a personal failing but a predictable outcome of systemic exploitation. Rest is not laziness; it is an act of defiance against a system that demands your constant labor while offering nothing in return. Education is also a powerful tool. While access to traditional education may be out of reach for many, free online resources and community learning programs can provide valuable skills and knowledge. Whether it's learning about labor rights, financial literacy, or a new trade, education empowers you to navigate and resist the systems that seek to keep you oppressed. Knowledge is not just power; it's survival.

As we navigate this corporate dystopia, it's essential to remember that the Reek regime's policies are not inevitable, they are choices made by those in power. And choices can be undone. Every act of resistance, every moment of solidarity, every effort to reclaim dignity in the workplace is a step toward dismantling this exploitative system. The Corporate Hunger Games may seem insurmountable, but history has shown us that when workers unite, they can topple even the most entrenched powers. It won't be easy, and it won't be quick, but the fight for fair and just labor conditions is a fight worth waging. The alternative is to accept a world where exploitation is the norm and survival is the only goal, and that is a future we must refuse to accept. Surviving the Corporate Hunger Games means more than enduring, it requires recalibrating how we think about work, value, and resistance. As deregulation deepens and labor protections erode further, the power dynamics of the workplace have tilted so heavily in favor of employers that the very notion of "rights" has become a relic. For women, particularly those in caregiving and low-wage roles, the stakes are even higher. This isn't just about making a living; it's about staying afloat in a system designed to sink you. In this second part, we'll explore how to navigate the increasingly hostile terrain of work under the Reek regime while laying the groundwork for resistance that challenges this exploitative structure.

The first reality to confront is that traditional pathways to workplace security, like collective bargaining or HR protections, are either crumbling or non-existent. Labor unions, long a bulwark against corporate overreach, are under siege. Anti-union laws, corporate intimidation tactics, and public disinformation campaigns have weakened unions to the point where only a fraction of workers are covered by collective agreements. For women in industries like caregiving or hospitality, where unions were already sparse, this leaves them more vulnerable than ever. Yet, even in this bleak landscape, union efforts are finding pockets of success, often led by workers themselves. Small victories, unionizing a single workplace, securing better wages for a specific group of workers, are lighting the way for others. If you're in a position to organize, know that it won't be easy, but it could be transformative.

For those in the gig economy, the struggle is even more fragmented. Gig work is intentionally designed to isolate workers from one another, preventing the kind of solidarity that leads to collective action. But cracks in this façade are beginning to show. Across the country, gig workers are forming grassroots organizations to demand better pay, safer conditions, and recognition as employees. Joining these efforts, even in small ways, attending meetings, signing petitions, or sharing experiences, can amplify the voices of those fighting for change. The algorithms may dictate your work, but they can't silence your humanity.

One of the most insidious consequences of deregulation is the normalization of exploitation. Long hours, unsafe conditions, and unpaid labor are framed as sacrifices you must make to succeed. This rhetoric is particularly harmful to women, who are often told to "lean in" and work harder to overcome systemic barriers. But leaning in when the system is stacked against you is not empowerment, it's entrapment. Instead, focus on identifying opportunities that genuinely align with your goals and values, even if they are unconventional. This might mean exploring freelance work, cooperative business models, or community-based enterprises that operate outside traditional corporate structures. It might also mean stepping back when the demands of work are threatening your well-being. Remember, your worth is not defined by your productivity.

Caregiving roles present their own set of challenges, and finding ways to survive in this sector requires creativity and collective action. Grassroots initiatives like caregiver cooperatives are gaining traction, providing fair wages, shared resources, and support networks for those in these demanding jobs. Advocating for state and local policies that support caregivers, like subsidies, tax credits, or grants, can also make a tangible difference. On an individual level, setting boundaries with employers and clients is crucial. Care work is emotionally and physically taxing, and without clear limits, burnout is inevitable.

Learn to say no, even when it feels uncomfortable. Your health and sanity are not negotiable. In industries where harassment and discrimination are rampant, documenting your experiences is a powerful tool. Keep records of incidents, conversations, and any retaliatory actions. These records may not prevent abuse in the moment, but they can provide leverage if you choose to file complaints or take legal action. Seek out advocacy organizations and legal aid groups that specialize in workplace rights. They can offer guidance, resources, and sometimes even representation. While the system may be stacked against you, you are not without recourse.

For those fortunate enough to have access to some measure of financial stability, consider using your resources to support broader efforts for change. This might mean donating to worker advocacy organizations, volunteering your time to teach financial literacy or workplace rights, or simply offering emotional support to those on the frontlines. Even small acts of solidarity can have ripple effects, building momentum for larger movements.

Beyond individual survival, it's essential to think about the long game. The Reek regime's policies are not immutable; they are the result of choices made by those in power. And choices can be reversed. Collective action, public pressure, and sustained advocacy have toppled oppressive systems before, and they can do so again. This means staying informed about labor issues, voting for candidates who prioritize worker rights, and supporting legislation that promotes equity and fairness in the workplace.

Technology also holds both challenges and opportunities in this fight. While corporations use algorithms and surveillance to control workers, those same tools can be turned against them. Social media platforms can amplify stories of abuse, rally support for strikes, and expose corporate malfeasance. Encrypted messaging apps and secure communication channels allow workers to organize without fear of retaliation. Learning how to use these tools effectively is a crucial part of modern resistance.

Ultimately, surviving the Corporate Hunger Games is about more than just getting by, it's about refusing to accept a system that dehumanizes and exploits. It's about demanding more than the bare minimum and working toward a future where labor is valued, dignity is protected, and exploitation is not the cost of survival. The road ahead is daunting, but the fight is necessary. Because no matter how ruthless the Reek regime's policies become, history has shown that workers, united, determined, and resilient, have the power to reshape the world. And that is a power no regime can take away.

The final layer of surviving the Corporate Hunger Games is about reclaiming your power, even in the face of a system designed to strip it away. The Reek regime's policies thrive on making workers feel small, disposable, and isolated, but the truth is that every worker holds immense collective potential. Part 3 is about embracing that potential and channeling it into meaningful resistance and long-term change.

First, understand that your labor is your leverage. Corporations rely on workers, even in a system tilted heavily in their favor. The key is finding ways to wield that leverage effectively. If unionizing is an option, support those efforts wholeheartedly, even if it seems risky. If it's not, look for alternative ways to disrupt the exploitative dynamics of your workplace. Organizing walkouts, demanding accountability, or even spreading awareness about mistreatment can begin to shift power dynamics. Remember, your silence is their greatest asset, don't give it to them.

Second, amplify voices fighting for systemic change. Individual survival is critical, but it's only part of the equation. Support local and national organizations pushing for policies like a higher minimum wage, universal healthcare, or stricter labor regulations. Share their messages, attend their events, and donate time or resources if you're able. The more visible the fight for workers' rights becomes, the harder it will be for the regime to ignore.

Third, redefine success on your own terms. The Reek regime and its corporate allies want you to believe that climbing their broken ladders is the only way forward. But success doesn't have to mean buying into their exploitative systems. Look for opportunities to build or join alternative economic models, like worker cooperatives, mutual aid networks, or community-supported businesses. These systems not only offer fairer conditions but also challenge the idea that profit should come before people.

Finally, nurture your resilience. This fight is a marathon, not a sprint, and burnout is a tool of the oppressor. Prioritize rest, build relationships that sustain you, and find joy wherever you can. Remember, survival in the Corporate Hunger Games isn't just about enduring, it's about resisting and reclaiming your humanity in the process. The odds may not seem in your favor, but history shows that when workers unite, even the most powerful regimes can be brought to their knees.

Checklist for Surviving the Corporate Hunger Games

Know Your Workplace Rights

Research labor laws in your state, including wage protections, safety standards, and anti-discrimination policies.

Familiarize yourself with federal laws that may still apply, such as protections against sexual harassment or retaliation for organizing.

Document Everything

Keep detailed records of hours worked, wages received, and any incidents of mistreatment or unsafe conditions.

Save emails, texts, and other communications with your employer, especially if they relate to disputes or complaints.

Connect with Worker Advocacy Groups

Seek out unions, local labor organizations, or advocacy groups in your industry. Even if unionizing isn't an option, these groups can provide resources, training, and support.

Foster Workplace Solidarity

Build connections with coworkers and encourage open dialogue about shared struggles. A united workforce is harder to exploit.

Share information about workplace rights and resources discreetly if necessary.

Learn to Navigate the Gig Economy

If you're working gig jobs, research platforms like Gig Workers Rising or Fairwork that provide guidance and advocacy for gig workers.

Track your earnings and expenses to ensure platforms are paying you fairly.

Protect Yourself from Retaliation

If you plan to report issues like harassment or wage theft, consult a legal aid organization for advice on minimizing risks.

Use secure, encrypted communication tools if organizing or discussing workplace issues could lead to retaliation.

Set Boundaries

Clearly define limits on your availability, workload, and responsibilities. Refuse unpaid overtime or tasks outside your job description if possible.

Prioritize your mental and physical health by recognizing when to step back or seek support.

Educate Yourself on Financial Literacy
Learn budgeting, saving, and debt management strategies to reduce financial dependence on exploitative jobs.
Explore side income options that align with your skills and values.

Explore Cooperative and Community Work Models
Research worker cooperatives or community-based businesses that emphasize fair wages, shared ownership, and equitable practices.
Consider forming your own cooperative with trusted colleagues if traditional employment options are exploitative.

Prepare for Job Loss or Transition
Keep your resume updated and learn new skills that increase your employability.
Build an emergency fund, even if it's small, to buffer against sudden job changes.

Support Broader Advocacy Efforts
Join campaigns or petitions that advocate for stronger labor protections and workplace rights.
Vote for candidates and policies that prioritize workers over corporate interests.

Stay Informed About Workplace Trends
Follow news and updates on labor issues, including automation, workplace surveillance, and industry-specific challenges.

The Ten Plagues of Project 2025
4~Climate Change for Thee, Not for Me

Climate change is no longer an abstract crisis looming on a distant horizon; it's here, and its impacts are devastating communities in ways that are both immediate and unrelenting. Under Project 2025, any semblance of climate action has been erased, replaced by policies designed to enrich the fossil fuel industry while sacrificing the planet and its people. The irony, of course, is that those who contribute the least to the climate crisis, women, children, and low-income families, are the ones who bear its heaviest burdens. Meanwhile, the architects of this disaster insulate themselves with wealth and privilege, building fortresses of convenience while leaving the rest of us to fend for ourselves.

Climate disasters, already increasing in frequency and intensity, are no longer anomalies but routine occurrences. Hurricanes, wildfires, droughts, and floods wreak havoc on a scale that feels apocalyptic, and the aftermath of each disaster exposes the deep inequalities baked into our systems. Women, especially those in caregiving roles, are often the first to shoulder the responsibility of recovery, whether it's finding shelter, securing food, or comforting children traumatized by the chaos. But what happens when the systems designed to support recovery, already strained by years of neglect, collapse entirely? Under the Reek regime, federal disaster relief has been gutted, leaving communities to scramble for resources on their own. Those with wealth can rebuild, relocate, and recover. Those without are left to endure.

Water shortages are becoming a grim reality in many parts of the country, as droughts intensify and water systems fail under the weight of climate stress and deregulation. For families already living paycheck to paycheck, the cost of bottled water or private well systems is an impossible burden. Women, often tasked with managing household needs, are forced to navigate the impossible math of deciding between water, food, and other necessities. The Reek regime, ever the servant of industry, has no qualms about privatizing water resources, handing control to corporations that prioritize profits over public access. The result? Entire communities cut off from the most basic of human rights: clean, affordable water.

Food insecurity is another escalating crisis, as climate change disrupts agricultural systems and creates sprawling food deserts. Crops fail, livestock perish, and supply chains crumble under the pressure of extreme weather events. For families in urban areas, access to fresh produce becomes a luxury, while rural communities find themselves grappling with skyrocketing prices for basic staples. The Reek regime's response has been predictable: dismantling food assistance programs and doubling down on policies that favor industrial agriculture over sustainable, community-based solutions. Women, as the primary caregivers in many households, bear the brunt of this crisis, often going without to ensure their children have something to eat.

In the face of these intersecting crises, adaptation becomes a necessity. But adaptation under Project 2025 is not the glossy, tech-driven transition to renewable energy we might have imagined. It's survival, plain and simple, and it often looks like a return to practices that prioritize resilience over convenience. Take diapers, for example. The rising costs of disposable products, coupled with supply chain disruptions, mean that reusable cloth diapers are making a resurgence, not as a trendy eco-friendly choice, but as a necessity for families who can no longer afford or access disposables. Similarly, backyard gardens and small-scale farming, once hobbies or side projects, are becoming critical lifelines for families trying to secure their own food.

Building resilience in the face of environmental collapse isn't just about meeting immediate needs; it's about preparing for a future where these crises are the norm, not the exception. This means rethinking how we approach housing, transportation, and community infrastructure. In the absence of federal leadership, grassroots efforts are stepping up to fill the void. Local organizations are developing community water banks, where neighbors share resources during shortages. Urban farming initiatives are turning vacant lots into productive gardens, providing fresh food and reducing dependence on corporate supply chains. These efforts, while inspiring, highlight the absurdity of a system where ordinary people are forced to do the work that governments should be leading.

For women, resilience also means navigating the unique challenges of caregiving during a climate crisis. It's not just about finding food and water; it's about managing the emotional toll that these crises take on families. Children, in particular, are deeply affected by the instability and uncertainty that come with environmental disasters. Helping them process their fears, maintain routines, and find moments of joy becomes another layer of responsibility for women already stretched thin. But this emotional labor, though exhausting, is a critical form of resilience. It ensures that even in the midst of collapse, humanity persists.

Yet, for all the personal adaptations we can make, it's impossible to ignore the systemic failures that make them necessary. Climate change is not a natural disaster; it's a man-made catastrophe driven by greed and negligence. The Reek regime's policies are not just passive failures to act, they are active contributors to the crisis. Deregulation of industries, the rollback of environmental protections, and the prioritization of corporate profits over planetary health have all accelerated the damage. And while individual actions can mitigate some of the impact, they are not enough to counter the scale of destruction being wrought by those in power.

The path forward is clear but daunting. It requires not just surviving the immediate crises but building a movement that demands systemic change. Women, who are disproportionately affected by climate change, are also uniquely positioned to lead this fight. History has shown that when women organize, they transform societies. From grassroots organizing to political advocacy, women are already at the forefront of climate justice movements, pushing for policies that prioritize equity, sustainability, and resilience. These movements recognize that climate change is not just an environmental issue; it's a social and economic one, deeply intertwined with issues of race, class, and gender.

As we navigate the early days of this climate dystopia, it's important to remember that resilience is not just about endurance, it's about imagination. It's about envisioning a future where the systems that caused this crisis are dismantled and replaced with ones that prioritize life over profit. It's about finding hope in the small acts of defiance that, when combined, have the power to create real change. And it's about refusing to accept the Reek regime's narrative that this is inevitable, that this is all there is. Because while the challenges ahead are immense, so too is our capacity to rise to them. This is not the end, it's the beginning of a fight that will define the generations to come.

The second layer of the climate crisis reveals the intricate web of vulnerabilities that Project 2025's policies have exacerbated, particularly for women and families. It's not just the immediate impact of disasters or shortages, it's the domino effect these events create, where one crisis sets off a chain reaction that ripples through every aspect of life. The Reek regime, for all its rhetoric about "stability" and "self-reliance," has built a world where the systems designed to protect people collapse under pressure, leaving individuals to pick up the pieces in a hostile and rapidly changing environment.

Take housing, for example. Climate change has rendered millions of homes uninhabitable, whether through floods, hurricanes, wildfires, or the slow creep of rising sea levels. In a just society, the government would step in with robust disaster relief programs, ensuring that displaced families have shelter and resources to rebuild. Instead, Project 2025 has gutted funding for programs like FEMA, turning disaster response into a patchwork of underfunded state initiatives and private charity. For low-income families, this often means long-term displacement, living in motels, shelters, or with relatives for months, sometimes years, while their wealthier counterparts rebuild quickly, thanks to private insurance and resources.

The housing crisis is further compounded by the deregulation of the rental market, allowing landlords and developers to exploit the scarcity of affordable housing. Women, particularly single mothers, are disproportionately affected, forced to accept substandard living conditions or spend an unsustainable portion of their income on rent. Evictions, already a crisis before climate change accelerated its toll, have skyrocketed in disaster-prone areas. Women juggling caregiving responsibilities and low-wage jobs find themselves at the mercy of a system that prioritizes profits over stability.

Transportation, another critical element of resilience, has also been undermined. In the wake of climate disasters, public transit systems are often among the first casualties, leaving communities stranded. Women who rely on buses, subways, or trains to commute to work, access healthcare, or buy groceries are left scrambling for alternatives. Meanwhile, the regime's policies have funneled resources into highways and infrastructure projects that benefit suburban and wealthy areas, further isolating those in urban and rural communities. Owning a car becomes less of a convenience and more of a necessity, but for many families, the rising cost of gas, insurance, and maintenance makes it unattainable.

Water shortages, already discussed as a pressing issue, carry a cascade of consequences that go beyond hydration. Women, particularly those in caregiving roles, must also think about cooking, cleaning, and sanitation. In regions where water is privatized or rationed, these responsibilities become grueling, time-consuming tasks. Imagine spending hours waiting in line at a distribution center for a few gallons of water, then carrying it home to ration it between meals, baths, and laundry. It's an exhausting reality that many women are already living, made worse by policies that prioritize industrial use of water over human needs.

Food insecurity continues to deepen as climate change destabilizes agricultural production. It's not just that crops are failing; it's that the entire food supply chain is collapsing under the weight of extreme weather and policy failures. Women in food deserts, where access to fresh produce was already limited, are now finding empty shelves and skyrocketing prices for the most basic staples. Feeding a family on a tight budget was hard enough before; now it's a daily battle against hunger, compounded by the emotional toll of trying to shield children from the full weight of the crisis.

In this context, the Reek regime's response has been predictable and cruel: blame the victims. Instead of addressing the systemic failures that leave families vulnerable, the regime leans on narratives of personal responsibility. If you're struggling, it's because you didn't prepare. If your home was destroyed, you should have moved. If you can't feed your kids, maybe you shouldn't have had them. These narratives are not just demoralizing; they are designed to deflect accountability from those in power while deepening the divisions that keep communities from organizing for change.

Despite these challenges, communities are finding ways to adapt and resist. Women are often at the forefront of these efforts, turning resourcefulness into an art form. Neighborhood water-sharing agreements, communal gardens, and barter systems are emerging as grassroots solutions to systemic failures. In some areas, women are organizing disaster preparedness groups, pooling knowledge and resources to protect their families and neighbors. These efforts are not just about survival; they are acts of defiance, a refusal to let the Reek regime's policies dictate the terms of their lives.

Resilience, however, is not just about adapting to the present, it's about preparing for a future that will demand even more from us. This means investing in skills and systems that increase self-sufficiency and reduce dependence on broken institutions. Learning to grow your own food, repair your home, and navigate local ecosystems for resources can make the difference between stability and collapse in a prolonged crisis. It also means teaching these skills to the next generation, ensuring that children grow up with the tools they need to face an uncertain future.

It's equally important to recognize that resilience is not just physical, it's emotional and psychological. Climate disasters take a toll on mental health, creating trauma that can linger long after the immediate danger has passed. Women, who often act as emotional anchors for their families, must find ways to process their own grief and fear while supporting others. This is no small task, but it's a crucial one. Building emotional resilience means creating spaces where women can share their experiences, seek support, and find moments of joy and connection amidst the chaos.

As daunting as these challenges are, they also offer an opportunity to reimagine what resilience looks like. The Reek regime's vision of survival is one of isolation and competition, where only the strong, or the wealthy, prevail. But true resilience is collective. It's about building systems that prioritize community, equity, and sustainability. It's about recognizing that the fight against climate change is also a fight against the inequalities that make its impacts so devastating. And it's about refusing to accept that the future has already been written. The Reek regime may have set the stage, but the story of how we respond is still ours to tell.

The third and final part of Climate Change for Thee, Not for Me shifts from the immediate challenges of survival to the larger question of how we build resilience not just to endure environmental collapse but to push back against the forces driving it. The Reek regime's climate policies are rooted in greed and willful ignorance, prioritizing corporate profits over human lives. But their actions have also laid bare the systemic failures that make their exploitation possible. In these cracks, there is room to grow something new, a movement built on equity, sustainability, and collective power.

Building resilience begins with acknowledging that climate change is not just an environmental issue, it is deeply intertwined with social, economic, and gender-based inequalities. Women, particularly those in caregiving roles, are often the first to adapt and respond during crises. This isn't a coincidence; it's a reflection of how systemic failures push the burden of survival onto those least equipped to bear it. But in this burden lies an opportunity. Women's resilience, creativity, and leadership are not just tools for survival, they are the foundation for transformative change.

One of the most powerful ways to fight back is by organizing at the community level. Large-scale policy changes may seem out of reach under the Reek regime, but local initiatives can still thrive. Community gardens, water-sharing cooperatives, and renewable energy projects are practical responses to immediate needs, but they also serve as models for a more sustainable future. By demonstrating that equitable and sustainable systems are not just possible but effective, these grassroots efforts challenge the legitimacy of the regime's extractive policies.

Education and skill-sharing are also critical components of resilience. In a world where institutions have failed, knowledge becomes one of the most valuable resources. Workshops on urban farming, water purification, first aid, and disaster preparedness can empower communities to take care of themselves and one another. Women, as the primary caregivers and often the most deeply embedded members of their communities, are uniquely positioned to lead these efforts. Sharing knowledge is not just an act of survival; it's an act of defiance against a regime that thrives on disempowerment.

At the same time, resilience must extend beyond practical skills to include emotional and psychological fortitude. Climate anxiety, grief, and trauma are real and debilitating, but they are also a shared experience that can bring people together. Support groups, storytelling circles, and creative outlets like art and music can help individuals process their emotions while building bonds of solidarity. Women, often the emotional anchors of their families and communities, play a critical role in fostering this kind of resilience.

Yet, while individual and community efforts are vital, they cannot replace systemic change. The Reek regime's policies are designed to make you believe that the climate crisis is your fault, that if only you recycled more, drove less, or used fewer plastic straws, the problem would be solved. This narrative is a lie. The crisis was created by corporations and governments that prioritized profit over the planet, and the only way to address it is to hold them accountable. This means joining or supporting climate justice movements that target the root causes of the crisis. It means amplifying the voices of those most affected, particularly Indigenous communities and people of color, who have long been at the forefront of the fight for environmental justice.

Resilience also requires reclaiming the political sphere, even when it feels impossible. Local elections, community boards, and grassroots campaigns may seem small compared to the scale of the climate crisis, but they are critical battlegrounds. These are the spaces where policies are made, resources are allocated, and change begins. Women, who are often underrepresented in these arenas, have the power to reshape them. Running for office, supporting female candidates, and advocating for equitable policies are all ways to build resilience not just for today but for the future.

Finally, resilience demands hope. This may seem counterintuitive in the face of environmental collapse, but hope is not a passive emotion, it's an active choice. It's the decision to believe that change is possible, even when the odds are stacked against you. It's the courage to imagine a better world and the determination to fight for it. The Reek regime wants you to feel defeated because despair keeps you compliant. Resilience means refusing to give them that power.

The climate crisis is overwhelming, but it is not insurmountable. Women have always been at the forefront of resistance movements, and this moment is no different. The challenges we face are immense, but so is our capacity to adapt, resist, and rebuild. Resilience is not just about surviving the storm; it's about using the storm's destruction to clear the way for something new. Together, we can build a future where equity, sustainability, and compassion are not afterthoughts but the foundation. This fight is far from over, and in that truth lies our greatest strength.

Checklist to Prepare for Climate Collapse

Secure Water Sources
Stockpile bottled water and invest in water filtration systems or portable purifiers.
Research local water-sharing cooperatives or community water banks.
Identify nearby natural water sources and learn basic purification techniques.

Grow or Source Your Own Food
Start a small garden, even if it's just a few containers on a balcony, to grow herbs, vegetables, or fruit.
Learn about community-supported agriculture (CSA) programs or local farmers' markets to access fresh, affordable produce.
Store non-perishable staples like grains, beans, and canned goods for emergencies.

Prepare Your Home for Disasters
Assess your home's vulnerabilities to floods, hurricanes, or wildfires and make necessary adjustments (e.g., sealing cracks, creating defensible space).
Build a disaster kit with essentials like flashlights, batteries, a first-aid kit, emergency blankets, and multi-purpose tools.

Strengthen Community Connections
Join local mutual aid groups or neighborhood associations focused on disaster preparedness.
Build relationships with neighbors to share resources and support during emergencies.

Learn Essential Skills
Take courses in first aid, basic repair, and survival skills like food preservation or foraging.

Learn how to grow food, collect rainwater, and use tools for DIY repairs.

Plan for Mobility and Evacuation

Identify multiple evacuation routes and establish a communication plan with family and friends.

Keep a "go bag" packed with essentials like ID, cash, food, water, medications, and a portable charger.

Advocate for Change

Support local climate justice initiatives and grassroots organizations working to address inequities in disaster response.

Push for policy changes in your community that prioritize sustainability and disaster resilience.

Invest in Renewable Energy and Efficiency

If possible, install solar panels or invest in other renewable energy sources for your home.

Replace appliances with energy-efficient options and improve insulation to reduce reliance on external systems.

Educate and Empower Others

Share resources and knowledge with your community, friends, and family to collectively prepare for and resist systemic failures.

Consider Relocating to Safer Areas

Research climate-resilient regions, such as areas with lower risks of wildfires, hurricanes, or rising sea levels.

Explore northern areas with more temperate climates and stable water resources as potential relocation options.

Plan for Potential Emigration

Investigate the immigration policies of countries with strong climate action plans and resilient infrastructure.

Secure passports and research the cost and logistics of relocating internationally if staying in the U.S. becomes unsustainable.

Learn Non-Technological Survival Skills

Practice skills like building shelters, making fires, foraging for food, and identifying safe plants and water sources.

Learn how to sew, mend, and repair items to reduce reliance on disposable goods and technology.

Develop Bartering and Trade Skills
Acquire practical skills such as gardening, herbal medicine, or crafting, which can be valuable in a barter economy.
Build relationships with others who possess complementary skills to establish mutual support networks.

Invest in Durable, Low-Tech Tools
Stock up on hand tools like manual can openers, saws, knives, and water-fetching equipment that don't require electricity or advanced technology.
Learn how to use and maintain these tools effectively.

Prepare for Long-Term Energy Independence
Research and invest in personal renewable energy sources, like portable solar panels or hand-crank generators.
Learn to live with minimal electricity by adapting your routines and finding alternatives for energy-dependent tasks.

Stock Up on Durable Clothing and Footwear
Invest in high-quality, weather-resistant clothing and boots suitable for various climates and conditions.
Learn to repair and care for your clothing to make it last longer.

Diversify Your Income Sources
Develop skills that allow you to work remotely or freelance, increasing your flexibility to move and adapt to changing conditions.
Consider side projects that can generate income or provide barter value, such as crafting, baking, or repair work.

Focus on Long-Term Mental and Physical Resilience
Build endurance and adaptability by regularly exercising, eating healthily, and practicing stress-management techniques.
Foster mental resilience by embracing uncertainty, maintaining optimism, and finding purpose in small daily actions.

The Ten Plagues of Project 2025
5~The War on Single Mothers

The War on Single Mothers is not a war waged in secret, it is a blatant, deliberate assault on the most vulnerable families in America. Under Project 2025, the safety nets designed to support single mothers and their children have been dismantled piece by piece, leaving millions to fend for themselves in an environment that punishes them for their circumstances. Welfare programs, childcare subsidies, housing assistance, lifelines that once offered a semblance of stability, are now relics of a past the Reek regime is determined to erase. In their place, we find punitive policies that criminalize poverty, shaming single mothers for needing help while denying them the tools to escape hardship. This war is not just economic; it is moral, cultural, and deeply gendered, targeting women and their children with a ferocity that lays bare the regime's priorities.

The death of welfare programs is at the center of this assault. The Reek regime's rhetoric frames public assistance as a drain on society, a handout for the lazy and undeserving. In reality, these programs have been a lifeline for countless single mothers trying to provide for their children in the face of systemic barriers. The dismantling of programs like Temporary Assistance for Needy Families (TANF) and the Supplemental Nutrition Assistance Program (SNAP) has plunged millions into food insecurity and financial ruin. For single mothers, who often juggle low-wage jobs with the demands of parenting, these cuts are devastating. The choice becomes stark: sacrifice your children's needs to keep a roof over their heads or risk losing everything.

Childcare subsidies, another crucial support system, have been slashed to the bone. For single mothers, affordable childcare is often the key to maintaining employment. Without it, the cost of daycare can exceed their monthly income, forcing them to leave the workforce entirely. The ripple effects are immediate and far-reaching: lost wages, lost opportunities for career advancement, and increased financial strain. The Reek regime's policies have turned childcare into an unattainable luxury for the wealthy, leaving working-class mothers scrambling for makeshift solutions that are neither safe nor sustainable.

Housing assistance, once a cornerstone of stability for low-income families, has also been gutted. The Department of Housing and Urban Development (HUD), now led by officials hostile to public housing, has slashed funding for Section 8 vouchers and public housing projects. As a result, single mothers face skyrocketing rents, substandard living conditions, and the constant threat of eviction. Homelessness among single-parent households, already a crisis before Project 2025, has reached catastrophic levels. Shelters are overwhelmed, leaving many families with no choice but to live in their cars or on the streets.

These cuts are not just cruel, they are strategic. By targeting single mothers, the Reek regime sends a clear message: poverty is a moral failing, not a systemic issue. The criminalization of poverty is perhaps the most insidious aspect of this war. Policies that penalize unpaid utility bills, truancy, or minor infractions disproportionately affect low-income families, turning everyday struggles into legal battles. For single mothers, the consequences are dire. Miss a rent payment? You could lose your home. Miss a court date? You might lose your kids. The system is designed to trap you, cycling families through a web of fines, fees, and legal obstacles that deepen their financial and emotional distress.

The criminal justice system plays a significant role in this cycle of oppression. Mothers who cannot afford childcare are often forced to bring their children to court appearances or legal proceedings, where their presence is met with disdain and judgment. If they are unable to pay court-ordered fees or fines, they risk incarceration, a punishment that separates them from their children and exacerbates their financial struggles. These policies are not just punitive; they are dehumanizing, reducing mothers to statistics in a system that profits from their suffering.

For women of color, the intersection of racism and misogyny magnifies these challenges. Black and Latina single mothers are disproportionately affected by cuts to welfare programs and housing assistance, as well as by the criminalization of poverty. The Reek regime's policies exploit existing racial inequalities, ensuring that the burden of these attacks falls heaviest on those already marginalized. This is not an unintended consequence; it is a deliberate strategy to maintain social hierarchies and deepen divisions among the working class.

Despite these overwhelming challenges, single mothers are finding ways to resist and rebuild. Solidarity among single-parent households is growing, as women recognize the power of collective action. Support networks, both formal and informal, are springing up across the country. These networks provide everything from childcare swaps to legal aid, creating a sense of community and shared purpose in a system that seeks to isolate them. Women are organizing protests, lobbying for policy changes, and challenging the narratives that frame them as unworthy of support. These acts of defiance, though often small in scale, are powerful reminders that resilience is not just about survival, it's about fighting back.

In addition to grassroots efforts, single mothers are also leveraging technology to connect and advocate for their needs. Social media platforms are being used to share resources, amplify stories, and organize campaigns. Online fundraisers help families avoid eviction, pay for medical bills, or cover childcare costs. These digital tools, while imperfect, provide a lifeline for mothers navigating a system designed to abandon them.

But solidarity alone is not enough. Building resilience in the face of systemic oppression requires addressing the root causes of poverty and inequality. This means pushing for policies that prioritize the needs of single mothers and their children, such as universal childcare, affordable housing, and living wages. It means challenging the cultural narratives that stigmatize public assistance and demand that mothers shoulder the burden of systemic failures alone. And it means holding the Reek regime accountable for its attacks on vulnerable families, refusing to let their cruelty go unchecked.

The War on Single Mothers is brutal, but it is not unwinnable. History is filled with examples of women rising up to demand justice for themselves and their families. This fight is no different. It will require courage, creativity, and an unshakable belief in the power of collective action. But in a world that seeks to divide and dehumanize, solidarity is the greatest weapon we have. Together, single mothers and their allies can build a future where no family is left behind, a future that prioritizes dignity, equality, and compassion over profit and punishment. The road will be long, but the stakes are too high to do anything less.

The second half of The War on Single Mothers delves deeper into how these systemic failures push single mothers into increasingly precarious situations, while also highlighting the strategies they are employing to fight back. The Reek regime's policies don't just strip away material resources; they erode the social fabric that single mothers rely on to survive and thrive. But even in the face of these relentless attacks, single mothers are demonstrating extraordinary resilience and ingenuity, finding ways to resist and rebuild.

One of the most devastating consequences of the regime's assault on single mothers is the rise in child welfare interventions. With safety nets like housing assistance and childcare subsidies dismantled, many single mothers find themselves unable to meet the arbitrary standards of "suitable" parenting imposed by child protective services. Families are torn apart not because mothers are neglectful or abusive, but because they lack the resources to provide stable housing or childcare. Once in the system, regaining custody of their children becomes a herculean task, requiring legal fees, court appearances, and compliance with impossible demands, all while struggling to keep a roof over their heads.

This weaponization of child welfare is not just a consequence of poverty; it's a tool of control. The Reek regime uses the fear of losing one's children to enforce compliance with their oppressive policies. Single mothers are less likely to challenge abusive landlords, exploitative employers, or unjust policies if doing so risks triggering a report to child protective services. This is a deliberate strategy to keep vulnerable families trapped in a cycle of dependency and fear.

In rural areas, the challenges are even more pronounced. The closure of local schools, hospitals, and childcare centers has turned vast swaths of the country into service deserts. Single mothers in these regions face insurmountable barriers to accessing even the most basic necessities. Public transportation is nonexistent, and the nearest resources may be hours away. The isolation imposed by geography is compounded by the stigma attached to asking for help, leaving many women to struggle alone. In urban areas, the story is different but no less harrowing. Gentrification, driven by deregulated housing markets, has pushed single mothers out of neighborhoods where they once had access to affordable housing, childcare, and community support. As rents skyrocket, families are forced into overcrowded apartments or unsafe living conditions. Meanwhile, wealthier residents enjoy the benefits of tax breaks and subsidies meant to attract development, a stark reminder of the regime's priorities.

In both urban and rural settings, single mothers are turning to alternative forms of support. Mutual aid networks, often organized by single mothers themselves, have become critical lifelines. These networks operate outside the traditional charity model, emphasizing solidarity over charity. Single mothers share childcare duties, swap goods and services, and pool resources to meet their collective needs. In doing so, they are not just surviving, they are creating communities built on trust, cooperation, and mutual respect.

One of the most powerful tools in these networks is knowledge-sharing. Single mothers are teaching one another how to navigate complex systems, from applying for remaining public assistance to fighting wrongful evictions. Legal aid workshops, financial literacy classes, and skill-sharing sessions are equipping women with the tools they need to advocate for themselves and their families. These grassroots efforts, while small in scale, are laying the groundwork for broader resistance. Technology is also playing a critical role in this fight. Online platforms allow single mothers to connect across geographic boundaries, share resources, and organize campaigns. Crowdfunding sites have become a vital resource for families facing eviction, medical emergencies, or unexpected expenses. Social media amplifies the voices of single mothers, turning individual stories of struggle into calls for collective action. These digital tools are not without their limitations, but they provide a much-needed counterbalance to the isolation imposed by the regime's policies.

Despite these efforts, the toll of navigating such a hostile system cannot be overstated. The emotional and psychological burden on single mothers is immense. Balancing work, parenting, and the constant fight for survival leaves little room for rest or recovery. Depression, anxiety, and burnout are common, but mental health services are increasingly out of reach. For many single mothers, the simple act of getting through the day feels like a victory in itself. Yet, even in this exhaustion, there is strength. Single mothers are not just enduring, they are fighting back. Advocacy groups led by single mothers are demanding policy changes at the local, state, and federal levels. They are lobbying for affordable housing, universal childcare, and expanded welfare programs. These movements recognize that the fight for single mothers' rights is inseparable from the broader fight for economic and social justice. It is a fight against a system that punishes poverty while rewarding exploitation, a system that values profit over people.

Building resilience also means redefining what success looks like for single mothers. The Reek regime's narrative frames them as failures, but their resilience, ingenuity, and strength tell a different story. Success is not about escaping poverty through sheer force of will, it's about challenging the systems that create and perpetuate it. It's about raising children who understand that their worth is not defined by their circumstances. It's about refusing to let the regime dictate the terms of your life.

As bleak as the War on Single Mothers may seem, history shows that change is possible when people come together to demand it. The welfare state itself was born out of struggle, built on the backs of women who refused to accept a world where their families were disposable. That struggle continues today, with single mothers leading the charge. They are not just victims of the Reek regime's policies, they are agents of change, fighting for a future where no family is left behind.

Checklist of Things Single Mothers Can Do to Prepare

Build a Local Support Network
Connect with neighbors, other single mothers, or local groups to share resources and childcare. A reliable community can provide emotional and practical support.

Research Available Resources
Familiarize yourself with food banks, legal aid, housing assistance, and other local programs.

Know Your Rights
Stay informed about your rights regarding housing, employment, and public assistance. Knowledge is power in a hostile system.

Create a Budget and Emergency Fund
Prioritize essentials like rent, food, and childcare, and save even small amounts for emergencies. Financial preparation provides a safety net during instability.

Prepare Important Documents
Keep birth certificates, medical records, school documents, and IDs in a safe, accessible place. Having these ready can streamline applications or emergencies.

Join Advocacy or Mutual Aid Groups
Connect with local or online groups that support single mothers. These networks provide resources, advocacy, and solidarity for navigating challenges.

Plan for Emergencies
Develop a plan for unexpected situations like eviction or job loss, including emergency contacts and shelters. Preparation reduces panic in crisis situations.

Focus on Physical and Mental Health
Prioritize your well-being with affordable exercise, nutritious food, and stress management practices. A healthy mind and body are crucial for resilience.

Teach Resilience to Your Kids
Involve children in age-appropriate planning and skill-building. Empowering them fosters confidence and teamwork within the family.

Leverage Technology
Use apps and online tools for budgeting, meal planning, and finding free or low-cost resources in your area. Technology can streamline daily challenges.

The Ten Plagues of Project 2025
6~Re-Education Camps for Kids AKA School

The transformation of schools into re-education camps under Project 2025 is one of the most insidious and far-reaching impacts of the Reek regime. Public education, once the bedrock of a functioning democracy, has been gutted in favor of a system that prioritizes religious indoctrination, censorship, and conformity. The goal is not to educate children to think critically or engage with the world in meaningful ways, it is to produce obedient citizens who accept authority without question. For parents, especially those who value science, empathy, and intellectual freedom, this presents an enormous challenge: how do you raise a generation of critical thinkers when the institutions designed to educate them have been co-opted by those who fear and punish critical thought?

The gutting of public education began with a systematic defunding of schools in favor of private, religious, and charter institutions. The rhetoric was cloaked in the language of "choice" and "freedom," but the reality is that this shift left millions of children, particularly those in low-income and rural areas, with underfunded schools that lack basic resources. Libraries are being closed, extracurricular programs canceled, and classrooms overcrowded. Teachers, already underpaid and overburdened, are fleeing the profession in droves, replaced by underqualified individuals who meet the ideological criteria of the regime rather than the pedagogical standards of education.

This crisis is particularly dire in schools where the curriculum has been rewritten to reflect the regime's priorities. Science classes now teach creationism alongside or instead of evolution. Climate change is either downplayed or framed as a hoax. History books are scrubbed of uncomfortable truths, replacing discussions of systemic inequality with sanitized narratives of national greatness. Sex education, if it exists at all, is reduced to abstinence-only programs that ignore the realities of consent, bodily autonomy, and reproductive health. Meanwhile, any mention of LGBTQ+ issues, racial justice, or alternative belief systems is banned outright, leaving children with a dangerously narrow and distorted understanding of the world.

The impacts of this re-education extend beyond academics. Schools are being transformed into ideological battlegrounds where dissent is not just discouraged but punished. Students are taught to accept authority uncritically, to view questioning as disobedience, and to equate patriotism with compliance. This shift isn't just about controlling what children learn, it's about shaping how they think, or rather ensuring that they don't think critically at all. The regime understands that a generation of critical thinkers is a threat to its power, and it has designed its education policies to neutralize that threat.

For parents, this dystopian shift presents a dual challenge: protecting their children from the harmful effects of this indoctrination while equipping them with the tools to resist it. The first step is recognizing the gaps in the education system and finding ways to fill them at home. This doesn't mean recreating a full curriculum, it means focusing on the areas that schools are failing to address. Teaching consent, for example, becomes a critical task for parents. Conversations about boundaries, respect, and bodily autonomy need to happen early and often, framed in ways that empower children to understand and assert their rights.

Science is another area where parents must step in. When schools teach pseudoscience or avoid critical topics altogether, it falls to families to foster curiosity and critical thinking. This might mean conducting simple experiments at home, visiting science museums, or encouraging kids to ask questions about the natural world. The goal is not just to provide facts but to teach children how to seek out reliable information, evaluate evidence, and think independently.

Empathy, too, must be cultivated at home. The regime's curriculum often erases or vilifies marginalized groups, perpetuating stereotypes and fostering intolerance. Parents can counteract this by exposing their children to diverse perspectives through books, films, and conversations. Encourage them to see the humanity in others, to understand different experiences, and to approach the world with compassion. These lessons are not just a counterbalance to the regime's agenda, they are acts of resistance in themselves.

While teaching at home is crucial, it's also important to recognize that parents cannot and should not do this work alone. Building a network of like-minded families can provide a support system for both parents and children. Study groups, book clubs, and co-ops can create spaces for kids to explore ideas that are banned or discouraged in their schools. These networks can also serve as a form of collective resistance, pushing back against the regime's policies through advocacy, protests, or even legal challenges.

Another critical strategy is teaching children how to navigate a world that punishes critical thought. This doesn't mean teaching them to hide their beliefs, it means helping them understand when and how to express themselves safely. Encourage them to ask questions, but also to recognize when it's better to stay silent. Teach them to seek out alternative sources of information, to think critically about what they're told, and to value evidence over rhetoric. These skills will not only help them survive the current system but also equip them to challenge it in the future.

Finally, parents must remember that raising critical thinkers is a long-term project. The impacts of the Reek regime's education policies will not be undone overnight, and the path forward will be fraught with challenges. But every conversation, every question, every act of resistance is a step toward reclaiming the future. The regime may control the schools, but it cannot control what happens in our homes, our communities, or our minds. And in that truth lies hope.

The second half of Re-Education Camps for Kids delves deeper into the tools, strategies, and long-term efforts parents can employ to ensure their children grow up as critical thinkers, despite the oppressive educational system imposed by Project 2025. The Reek regime's attempt to control the minds of the next generation is rooted in fear, fear of dissent, fear of change, and fear of empowered individuals who question their authority. To counter this, parents must cultivate resilience, curiosity, and courage in their children, planting the seeds of resistance that will eventually blossom into transformative change.

One of the first challenges parents face is counteracting the regime's sanitized, heavily censored version of history. Textbooks have become tools of propaganda, erasing uncomfortable truths about racism, colonialism, and systemic inequality. In their place are narratives that glorify conquest, celebrate obedience, and minimize the struggles of marginalized groups. To combat this, parents must take on the role of historians, introducing their children to the voices and stories that the regime has erased. Libraries, independent bookstores, and online archives are invaluable resources for finding materials that present a fuller, more honest account of history.

Conversations about history should also include discussions about power, who holds it, how it's used, and why it's often abused. Encourage your children to question why certain events are portrayed in specific ways and whose perspectives are missing from the narrative. Teaching them to analyze history critically helps them understand the present and equips them to navigate the future with clarity and confidence.

Another critical area of focus is media literacy. The regime's control extends beyond schools to the media landscape, where misinformation and propaganda are rampant. Teaching children how to evaluate sources, recognize bias, and differentiate between facts and opinions is essential. Encourage them to question everything they see and hear, whether it's on TV, in a classroom, or on social media. Introduce them to reputable, independent news outlets and discuss current events together, fostering a habit of informed, thoughtful engagement with the world.

Creativity is another powerful tool for resisting indoctrination. Art, music, and storytelling allow children to explore their identities, express their emotions, and imagine alternative futures. In a world that punishes critical thought, creativity is both a refuge and a weapon. Encourage your children to write stories, draw pictures, or compose songs that reflect their ideas and experiences. Expose them to diverse forms of art and literature that challenge conventional norms and expand their understanding of the world.

Building a sense of agency is equally important. The regime's educational policies are designed to instill helplessness, teaching children that their roles are to follow orders and accept the status quo. Parents can counter this by involving their children in decision-making processes at home. Let them have a say in family rules, meal planning, or weekend activities. Encourage them to take on small responsibilities and celebrate their successes. These experiences teach children that their voices matter and that they have the power to shape their lives.

Community involvement is another avenue for fostering critical thinking and resilience. While schools may be failing, community organizations, libraries, and local groups can provide opportunities for children to engage with ideas and activities that nurture their intellectual growth. Look for book clubs, science workshops, or volunteer programs that align with your values and allow your children to connect with others who share their interests.

Parents must also prepare their children for the inevitable challenges of growing up in a world that punishes dissent. Teaching them emotional resilience is key. Help them develop healthy coping mechanisms for dealing with frustration, fear, or disappointment. Create a safe space at home where they can express their thoughts and feelings without judgment. Encourage them to approach challenges with a problem-solving mindset, seeing obstacles not as insurmountable barriers but as opportunities for growth and learning.

Additionally, teach children the value of solidarity. The regime's policies thrive on isolation, fostering an environment where individuals feel alone in their struggles. Show your children the importance of standing with others, whether it's through small acts of kindness or larger acts of resistance. Teach them to recognize injustice not just in their own lives but in the lives of others and to understand that collective action is often the most effective way to create change.

Finally, remember that raising critical thinkers is not just about countering the regime's policies, it's about preparing children to build a better world. Encourage them to dream big and think boldly about the future they want to see. Support their passions, nurture their talents, and remind them that their voices can make a difference. While the Reek regime may control the present, it is the next generation that will shape the future.

In the end, the most powerful tool parents have is love. The Reek regime's policies are rooted in fear, but love is stronger than fear. Love for your children, for truth, and for a better future is what drives the fight against indoctrination. By fostering critical thought, creativity, and resilience in your children, you are not just helping them survive, you are helping them thrive. Together, we can resist the regime's efforts to control our minds and build a world where education is a tool for empowerment, not oppression.

The final piece of Re-Education Camps for Kids focuses on long-term strategies for resisting the regime's control of education and ensuring that the seeds of critical thinking and empowerment planted today continue to grow into the future. While the challenges of raising children under Project 2025 are immense, this part emphasizes the importance of resilience, community, and hope in building a generation that can resist indoctrination and eventually dismantle the systems that oppress them.

A key long-term strategy is fostering curiosity as a lifelong habit. Critical thinking doesn't end when a child leaves the classroom; it's a skill that must be nurtured continuously. Encourage children to ask "why" and "how" about everything they encounter, from science experiments to social systems. Support their interests, even if they don't align with traditional academic subjects, and provide opportunities for them to explore their passions. A child who is deeply engaged in the world around them is harder to control and more likely to resist simplistic narratives.

Another essential element is teaching children how to identify and challenge injustice. Start small, with discussions about fairness in everyday situations, and gradually expand those conversations to include larger social issues. Role-playing can be an effective way to practice standing up to authority figures or challenging peers in a constructive way. Children who understand that their voices matter, and who have practiced using them, are more likely to speak out when it truly counts.

At the same time, parents must prepare their children for the potential risks of dissent in an increasingly authoritarian world. Teach them how to navigate systems that punish critical thought without compromising their values. This might mean learning how to express themselves in ways that fly under the radar or knowing when it's safer to stay silent. Equip them with tools for secure communication, like encrypted messaging apps, and emphasize the importance of documenting injustices while protecting their privacy.

Community remains a cornerstone of long-term resistance. Encourage your children to build strong, supportive relationships with peers who share their values. Friendships based on mutual respect and shared purpose are not just a source of comfort, they're a foundation for collective action. Consider organizing study groups or extracurricular activities that allow kids to explore banned ideas and develop critical thinking in a safe, collaborative environment.

Finally, emphasize hope. The Reek regime wants children to believe that resistance is futile, that the world is unchangeable, and that their actions don't matter. Counter this narrative by sharing stories of successful resistance movements from history and by celebrating even small victories in their own lives. Remind them that the future is not set in stone and that they have the power to shape it.

In raising critical thinkers under an oppressive system, parents are not just preparing their children to survive, they are preparing them to lead. By fostering curiosity, resilience, and a sense of justice, you are equipping the next generation to challenge the status quo and build a world where education is a tool for liberation, not control. This is the ultimate act of defiance and the greatest legacy we can leave for our children.

Books to Navigate Authoritarianism

For Kids

The Giver by Lois Lowry
A thought-provoking tale about a controlled society and the value of individual freedom and memory.

One Crazy Summer by Rita Williams-Garcia
Set in the 1960s, this novel follows three sisters sent to spend the summer with their mother, a member of the Black Panther Party, exploring themes of activism, justice, and standing up against systemic oppression.

The Hunger Games by Suzanne Collins (Young Adult)
Explores themes of rebellion, oppression, and the power of collective action.

When Hitler Stole Pink Rabbit by Judith Kerr
A child's perspective on fleeing authoritarianism and finding hope in uncertainty.

Roll of Thunder, Hear My Cry by Mildred D. Taylor
Set in the Jim Crow South, this novel tackles systemic racism, injustice, and the importance of family and community.

Harriet the Spy by Louise Fitzhugh
Encourages kids to question their surroundings and think critically about the world.

I Am Malala (Young Readers Edition) by Malala Yousafzai
A memoir of standing up for education and equality in the face of oppression.

Anne Frank: The Diary of a Young Girl
A personal account of living under authoritarian rule and finding hope in humanity.

Esperanza Rising by Pam Muñoz Ryan
A story of resilience, adaptability, and strength in the face of systemic oppression.

Maus (Graphic Novel) by Art Spiegelman (Teens and Adults)
A powerful graphic novel about survival, resistance, and the intergenerational impact of authoritarianism.

For Adults

1984 by George Orwell
A seminal work on surveillance, propaganda, and the dangers of totalitarianism.

The Origins of Totalitarianism by Hannah Arendt
A deep dive into how authoritarian regimes rise and sustain power.

On Tyranny: Twenty Lessons from the Twentieth Century by Timothy Snyder
A concise, actionable guide for resisting authoritarianism.

Brave New World by Aldous Huxley
A cautionary tale about the dangers of losing individuality to authoritarian control disguised as comfort.

It Can't Happen Here by Sinclair Lewis
A chilling portrayal of how authoritarianism could take hold in the United States.

The Handmaid's Tale by Margaret Atwood
A dystopian exploration of gender, power, and control under a theocratic regime.

How Democracies Die by Steven Levitsky and Daniel Ziblatt
Analyzes the warning signs of democratic backsliding and authoritarian creep.

Persepolis (Graphic Memoir) by Marjane Satrapi
A personal account of growing up under an authoritarian regime in Iran.

Animal Farm by George Orwell
An allegorical critique of authoritarianism and the corruption of revolutionary ideals.

The Ministry for the Future by Kim Stanley Robinson
A speculative fiction novel that explores the intersection of climate crisis, authoritarianism, and global resistance, providing a hopeful yet critical look at how humanity might address systemic challenges.

Twilight of Democracy: The Seductive Lure of Authoritarianism by Anne Applebaum
Explores how and why people are drawn to authoritarian regimes, examining the societal fractures, cultural shifts, and political dynamics that enable the rise of illiberalism.

Fahrenheit 451 by Ray Bradbury
A dystopian exploration of censorship and the suppression of dissenting ideas.

Why Civil Resistance Works: The Strategic Logic of Nonviolent Conflict by Erica Chenoweth and Maria J. Stephan

A study of how nonviolent resistance has historically succeeded against authoritarian regimes.

They Thought They Were Free: The Germans, 1933–45 by Milton Mayer
Examines how ordinary people came to accept and participate in an authoritarian regime.

The Shock Doctrine: The Rise of Disaster Capitalism by Naomi Klein
An exploration of how authoritarian regimes exploit crises to consolidate power.

Checklist to Prepare for Re-Education Camps for Kids

Teach Critical Thinking at Home
Encourage your children to ask questions, evaluate evidence, and think independently about what they're taught in school.

Build a Home Library
Stock up on books that promote critical thought, diverse perspectives, and historical accuracy to counteract biased school curricula.

Supplement Their Education
Teach science, history, and social issues at home, filling gaps left by a censored curriculum. Consider hands-on experiments and discussions.

Focus on Emotional Intelligence
Help your children develop empathy, resilience, and communication skills to navigate a divisive educational environment.

Discuss Media Literacy
Teach your kids to recognize bias, verify sources, and critically evaluate the information they consume online and offline.

Join or Form Parent Groups
Connect with like-minded parents to share resources, organize extracurricular learning opportunities, and advocate for better educational policies.

Monitor School Policies
Stay informed about changes in school curriculum and policies, and advocate for transparency and accountability in educational content.

Encourage Creativity
Support art, writing, and other creative outlets to give your kids a way to express themselves and process the world around them.

Introduce Diverse Perspectives
Use books, documentaries, and conversations to expose your children to global cultures, histories, and viewpoints suppressed in their school environment.

Teach Consent and Autonomy
Have ongoing discussions about personal boundaries, bodily autonomy, and the importance of respecting others' rights, countering abstinence-only narratives.

Prepare for Discussions on Taboo Topics
Be ready to address subjects like climate change, LGBTQ+ rights, and racial justice, as these may be excluded or misrepresented in school.

Encourage Safe Advocacy
Teach your children how to express their views thoughtfully and when it's appropriate to challenge authority or stay silent for safety.

Use Technology Wisely
Leverage educational apps and online resources to provide well-rounded learning and ensure access to accurate information.

Support Their Peer Relationships
Help your children form connections with peers who value critical thinking and mutual respect, building a network of like-minded allies.

Teach Resilience and Adaptability
Prepare your children to navigate challenging environments while holding onto their values and intellectual curiosity.

The Ten Plagues of Project 2025
7~Patriarchy, Now with Extra Testosterone

Under Project 2025, the patriarchy isn't just reinforced, it's turbocharged, embedded into every corner of life, from the highest levels of government to the most intimate dynamics of the home. The Reek regime's policies and cultural agenda make no effort to hide their priorities: the systematic subjugation of women and the glorification of male dominance as the "natural" order of things. At the core of this vision is a revival of rigid gender roles, with women relegated to caregiving and reproductive duties while men assume control of leadership, resources, and decision-making. This isn't patriarchy as we've always known it, it's patriarchy on steroids, with extra testosterone fueling its oppressive machinery.

The first arena where this male-dominated hierarchy is glaringly obvious is in government. Across federal, state, and local levels, male leadership dominates like never before, as the regime prioritizes appointing men to critical positions while sidelining, silencing, or outright removing women from the halls of power. Women leaders who dare to question the regime's agenda are branded as unfit, emotional, or radical, their voices drowned out by a chorus of old boys' club rhetoric. Laws governing reproductive rights, workplace protections, and family policy are crafted almost exclusively by men, men who will never face the consequences of the restrictions they impose. Decisions about women's bodies, lives, and futures are made without their input, reducing half the population to spectators in a game that directly affects their survival.

This same dynamic seeps into the workplace, where Project 2025's rollback of gender equity policies erases decades of progress. Pay gaps widen as enforcement of equal pay laws disappears. Workplace harassment becomes normalized as oversight agencies are defunded or neutered, leaving women with little recourse against discriminatory practices. The so-called "glass ceiling" is reinforced with iron bars, barring women from leadership roles and opportunities for advancement. Meanwhile, male-dominated industries thrive, propped up by tax breaks and deregulation, while traditionally female-led sectors like education, healthcare, and social services are underfunded and undervalued. For women trying to balance work and family, the collapse of childcare subsidies and workplace accommodations makes career growth nearly impossible. The result is a labor market that systematically drives women out, punishes ambition, and rewards compliance with patriarchal norms.

The home, long considered a private refuge, has become another battlefield in the Reek regime's war on women's autonomy. Policies that undermine divorce laws, reduce access to domestic violence resources, and promote traditional family structures trap women in abusive or unbalanced relationships. Men are encouraged to assert dominance in the household, framed as "protectors" and "providers" while women are cast as submissive caretakers. Cultural messaging reinforces this dynamic, with propaganda glorifying the "traditional wife" as the ideal, shaming women who seek independence, and stigmatizing those who challenge gender norms. This deliberate erosion of equality in personal relationships serves the regime's broader agenda: keeping women disempowered, isolated, and dependent.

The regime's policies don't just treat women as second-class citizens, they actively punish those who resist this status. Women who speak out against injustice, whether in politics, workplaces, or their communities, are labeled as troublemakers or threats to social order. Activism is met with harsh crackdowns, from online harassment campaigns to legal repercussions. The Reek regime has weaponized the very systems that should protect women, turning them into tools of control. Law enforcement, for instance, often dismisses or diminishes reports of gender-based violence, leaving women vulnerable and without recourse. Courts, heavily influenced by conservative ideology, make rulings that prioritize male authority, whether in custody battles, property disputes, or workplace discrimination cases.

This oppressive environment demands a multifaceted approach to empowerment and resistance. The first step is acknowledging the reality of this new patriarchy and understanding its mechanisms. Women must recognize the systemic nature of their oppression and refuse to internalize the narratives that blame them for their circumstances. The Reek regime thrives on convincing women that they are inadequate, undeserving, or powerless, but these are lies meant to maintain control. Rejecting these narratives is an act of defiance in itself.

Building networks of solidarity is another critical strategy. In a world designed to isolate and silence women, connections with like-minded individuals become lifelines. Women's groups, mutual aid networks, and advocacy organizations offer spaces for support, resource-sharing, and collective action. These networks are particularly vital in challenging the regime's cultural messaging, providing platforms for alternative narratives that celebrate women's strength, diversity, and contributions. They also serve as hubs for resistance, organizing protests, campaigns, and legal challenges to counteract oppressive policies.

Resilience in the workplace requires adaptability and strategic thinking. Women can protect their autonomy by diversifying their skill sets, seeking out mentors, and building professional networks that prioritize mutual support over competition. While the system may be rigged, these connections can provide access to opportunities and resources that help women navigate its challenges. Additionally, understanding workplace rights, even as they are eroded, empowers women to advocate for themselves and push back against exploitation.

In the home, empowerment means reclaiming agency in personal relationships. Open communication, boundary-setting, and mutual respect are essential for challenging traditional power dynamics. Women must also be prepared to recognize and address signs of unhealthy or abusive behavior, seeking support from trusted friends, family, or organizations when necessary. For those raising children, this also means modeling equality, empathy, and critical thinking, teaching the next generation to reject the patriarchal norms that the Reek regime seeks to enforce.

Finally, staying empowered requires a commitment to self-care and mental health. Living under an authoritarian patriarchy is exhausting, and the regime's policies are designed to wear women down. Prioritizing well-being, whether through therapy, creative outlets, or simply carving out time for rest, is not a luxury; it is a survival strategy. Resilience is built not just through action but through restoration, ensuring that women have the strength to continue fighting.

The Reek regime's vision of a male-dominated society may be oppressive, but it is not inevitable. Women have faced and resisted patriarchal systems throughout history, and this moment is no different. The strategies outlined here, understanding, connecting, adapting, and caring, are the building blocks of resistance. By refusing to accept the roles imposed on them, women can challenge the very foundations of the regime's power. And in doing so, they can create a future where empowerment is not an act of defiance but a fundamental right.

The second half of Patriarchy, Now With Extra Testosterone focuses on actionable strategies for women to reclaim their agency and resist systemic oppression under Project 2025's hyper-patriarchal policies. While the Reek regime's vision of male dominance infiltrates every sphere of life, history shows that no system of oppression is unshakable. Empowerment, resilience, and collective action remain powerful tools for dismantling even the most entrenched forms of inequality.

One of the first and most critical strategies for resisting this amplified patriarchy is education, both formal and informal. Education has always been a pathway to empowerment, but under a regime that seeks to control knowledge and enforce ideological conformity, it becomes an act of rebellion. Women must actively seek out opportunities to expand their knowledge, whether through online courses, local workshops, or self-directed study. Topics like financial literacy, legal rights, advocacy, and self-defense are particularly crucial, equipping women with the skills to navigate and challenge a system stacked against them.

Parents, especially mothers, have a unique role in countering the regime's patriarchal agenda by teaching their children values that contradict the imposed norms. Raising boys who respect equality and reject toxic masculinity is a profound form of resistance. Similarly, empowering girls to see themselves as capable, independent, and deserving of equal opportunities lays the foundation for a generation that will push back against systemic sexism. These lessons can be woven into everyday life, through the books they read, the stories they hear, and the behaviors they see modeled by the adults around them.

Collective action remains one of the most effective ways to resist patriarchy. Throughout history, women's movements have achieved monumental progress through organizing and solidarity, and that same power exists today. Joining or forming local advocacy groups, women's networks, or mutual aid collectives can provide both support and a platform for meaningful action. These groups can lobby for policy changes, raise awareness about issues affecting women, and offer resources to those in need. Collective action not only amplifies individual voices but also builds community, creating a sense of solidarity that is vital in the face of systemic oppression.

Economic empowerment is another crucial area of focus. Financial independence has always been a cornerstone of women's liberation, and it becomes even more critical under a regime that seeks to enforce dependency. Women should prioritize developing skills and pursuing opportunities that enhance their earning potential, even in a hostile job market. This might mean learning new trades, starting side businesses, or investing in certifications that open up higher-paying roles. Diversifying income streams and building financial resilience not only helps women protect themselves but also weakens the regime's grip on economic power.

The workplace, while often a site of exploitation under patriarchal systems, can also be a place of resistance. Women can build networks within their industries to support one another, share resources, and advocate for better conditions. Mentorship programs, professional organizations, and peer groups are powerful tools for navigating male-dominated spaces. While the regime may attempt to strip away workplace protections, women who band together can create their own systems of accountability and mutual aid, challenging exploitative practices from within.

In the home, challenging patriarchal dynamics means reclaiming agency and fostering equality in personal relationships. For women in partnerships, this involves open communication about roles, responsibilities, and decision-making. Setting boundaries and advocating for mutual respect are key steps in disrupting traditional power imbalances. Women in abusive or controlling relationships may face greater barriers, particularly as the Reek regime dismantles resources for survivors of domestic violence. In these cases, reaching out to trusted networks or underground support organizations becomes essential for safety and empowerment.

Art and storytelling are underutilized but powerful tools in the fight against patriarchy. Women have always used creativity to challenge societal norms, and under Project 2025, art becomes both a refuge and a weapon. Writing, painting, filmmaking, and other forms of expression provide a means to document experiences, share ideas, and inspire action. Public art projects, zines, and online storytelling platforms can counter the regime's propaganda, reminding women that their voices and perspectives matter. Creativity also has the power to build community, connecting women through shared experiences and collective imagination.

Spirituality and self-care are equally important in resisting patriarchy. The Reek regime's vision of a male-dominated society thrives on wearing women down, physically, emotionally, and mentally. Practices like mindfulness, meditation, journaling, and connecting with nature can help women reclaim a sense of control over their inner lives. Spiritual communities, when inclusive and supportive, can also offer a source of strength and belonging, countering the isolation imposed by patriarchal systems.

Finally, women must embrace the long game. Dismantling patriarchy is not a quick or easy process, especially under a regime that has embedded it into every institution. Resilience and persistence are critical, as is a willingness to adapt strategies as circumstances change. It's important to celebrate small victories, whether it's helping a single mother find housing, supporting a coworker through a workplace dispute, or simply holding space for a friend who feels silenced. These acts of solidarity may seem minor, but they contribute to a larger culture of resistance that cannot be extinguished.

The Reek regime's patriarchy, though deeply entrenched, is not invincible. Women's voices, actions, and collective power have toppled oppressive systems before, and they can do so again. By prioritizing education, building networks of solidarity, fostering financial independence, and nurturing their well-being, women can reclaim their agency and challenge the structures designed to suppress them. This is not just a fight for survival, it is a fight for liberation, equality, and the right to live fully and freely. And it is a fight worth waging.

Patriarchy: From History to Weaponized Tool

Ancient Origins (10,000 BCE – 476 CE):
Patriarchy emerged with the advent of agricultural societies, where landownership and inheritance prioritized male dominance. Over centuries, male-dominated structures were institutionalized in law, religion, and governance, reinforcing the view of women as property and secondary to men.

The Middle Ages (476 – 1500 CE):
Religious institutions played a central role in deepening patriarchal norms. Women were excluded from leadership, and their roles were confined to childbearing, caregiving, or cloistered religious service. Religious texts and dogma were weaponized to justify control over women's bodies and autonomy.

Industrial Revolution (1700s – 1800s):
Patriarchy adapted to economic systems, as industrialization relegated women to low-wage labor or domestic roles while men controlled the wealth and power of emerging capitalist societies. Movements for women's suffrage and rights began to challenge these systems.

20th Century: Push and Pull (1900s):
The fight for equality gained momentum with milestones like women's suffrage, reproductive rights, and workplace protections. Yet, patriarchal systems continued to adapt, maintaining dominance through wage gaps, discriminatory laws, and cultural norms.

The Rise of Religious Nationalism (1980s – 2000s):
Patriarchy intertwined with political agendas, particularly in the United States. Conservative religious movements framed gender roles as divinely mandated, using legislation and rhetoric to push back against progress in women's rights.

Project 2025: Patriarchy as a Weapon (2025 Onward):
In the Reek regime's America, patriarchy becomes an overt tool of authoritarianism, weaponized to enforce religious zealotry and fascist

control. Women's bodies, roles, and lives are subjected to extreme surveillance and control, justified by twisted interpretations of "family values" and biblical mandates. Patriarchy is no longer just a social structure, it's a strategic means to suppress dissent, consolidate power, and maintain a rigid hierarchy where white, male dominance is absolute.

Under Project 2025, patriarchy is institutionalized into law, stripping women of autonomy, silencing their voices, and turning their oppression into a pillar of the regime's identity. Resistance, then, becomes not just a fight against sexism, but a battle for democracy, freedom, and the right to exist on one's own terms.

Checklist to Prepare for and Resisting Patriarchy

Educate Yourself on Gender Rights and Policies

Learn about your legal rights regarding workplace discrimination, reproductive health, and personal safety. Stay informed about new laws and policies that may impact you.

Build a Support Network

Connect with like-minded women, allies, and advocacy groups to share resources, experiences, and strategies for resistance.

Teach Equality at Home

Model and teach values of equality, respect, and mutual responsibility to children. Challenge traditional gender roles through conversations and actions.

Prioritize Financial Independence

Invest in skills or certifications to increase earning potential. Create a budget, build an emergency fund, and explore income diversification strategies.

Join or Form Advocacy Groups

Participate in or establish local women's groups to fight for policy changes, provide mutual aid, and create safe spaces for dialogue and support.

Support and Mentor Other Women
Actively lift up other women in your community or workplace by sharing opportunities, offering guidance, and creating pathways for mutual success.

Push Back Against Workplace Inequities
Document incidents of discrimination or harassment and know how to escalate issues if necessary. Build alliances with coworkers to challenge unfair practices.

Prepare for Personal Safety
Take self-defense classes and learn how to recognize and safely exit abusive or controlling relationships. Keep important contacts and resources readily available.

Empower Yourself Through Knowledge
Read books, attend workshops, or take courses on feminism, gender equity, and resistance strategies to strengthen your understanding and advocacy skills.

Foster Resilience Through Self-Care
Prioritize your mental and physical health through regular rest, mindfulness practices, and creative outlets to counter the draining effects of systemic oppression.

Challenge Cultural Narratives
Use art, storytelling, and conversations to counteract patriarchal propaganda. Share stories of resilience, equality, and resistance to inspire others.

Raise Awareness in Your Community
Host discussions, book clubs, or workshops that highlight the impacts of patriarchy and offer actionable steps for change.
Keep records of injustices you or others face. Use social media or local platforms to amplify these issues and call for accountability.

Promote and Support Women in Leadership
Vote for women leaders, support women-owned businesses, and advocate for policies that ensure fair representation in government and workplaces.

The Ten Plagues of Project 2025
8~Policing Women's Bodies

Under Project 2025, women's bodies have become the frontline of a terrifying and calculated system of control, merging authoritarianism, surveillance, and societal policing into a singular apparatus of oppression. This is not merely a resurgence of historical patterns of subjugation but their reconfiguration into a modern state apparatus designed to strip women of autonomy and agency. Women are no longer seen as individuals with inherent rights over their bodies but as subjects whose choices must align with the regime's narrow vision of morality and order. This deliberate and systemic effort transforms personal decisions into matters of public judgment and enforcement, embedding these controls into law, culture, and community. Under this regime, autonomy is not seen as a right but as a privilege, tightly controlled and easily revoked by a government bent on entrenching patriarchal power.

Among the most blatant mechanisms of control are the laws restricting women's ability to travel for reproductive healthcare. Historically, the right to travel and seek medical care across state lines has been a fundamental freedom, rooted in the recognition that healthcare access should not be determined by geography or political ideology. However, Project 2025 has weaponized this freedom against women by supporting laws like Idaho's so-called "abortion trafficking" law, which criminalizes individuals who assist minors in obtaining abortion care out of state without parental consent. These laws do more than limit access; they create an environment of fear and suspicion, deterring individuals from offering support to those seeking care. Women are effectively trapped within the borders of their states, where access to safe and legal abortion services may be nonexistent. For many, particularly those in rural or conservative areas, the inability to travel for healthcare transforms pregnancy into a life-threatening ordeal, one where the state's interest in controlling reproduction overrides the individual's right to life and health.

These travel restrictions are exacerbated by the pervasive influence of laws like Texas's Senate Bill 8, the infamous "bounty law." This legislation deputizes private citizens to sue anyone who assists in providing or obtaining an abortion after six weeks of pregnancy, incentivizing them with financial rewards of at least $10,000 per successful lawsuit. The implications of this law are chilling. It effectively transforms ordinary citizens into enforcers of state policies, fostering a culture of surveillance and mistrust where neighbors, coworkers, and even family members may report one another for perceived infractions. Healthcare providers, already operating under tremendous pressure and scrutiny, are deterred from offering care for fear of litigation, while individuals who might otherwise support women seeking abortions hesitate, knowing they too could become targets of legal action. The normalization of citizen surveillance is a deliberate strategy to erode solidarity, replacing communal support with suspicion and fear. This law is not just a tool for controlling access to abortion; it is a cultural weapon designed to fracture communities and isolate women.

The criminalization of abortion reaches its most extreme form in the framing of abortion as murder. States like South Carolina have introduced legislation proposing that abortion be treated as homicide, with penalties that could include life imprisonment or even the death penalty for women who terminate pregnancies. While such laws have not yet been universally enacted, their existence signals a radical shift in how the state views women's bodies and reproductive rights. By granting embryos and fetuses the same legal rights as living individuals, these measures render women's bodies subordinate to the state's interpretation of morality and justice. The implications are profound: miscarriages can be treated as potential crimes, requiring women to prove their innocence; medical professionals are deterred from offering care that could be perceived as aiding abortion; and women are forced to endure pregnancies against their will, regardless of the risks to their physical and emotional health. This shift fundamentally redefines the relationship between women and the state, positioning the latter as the ultimate arbiter of what happens within a woman's body.

Technology, once seen as a tool for empowerment, has been weaponized in this new regime to further erode women's autonomy. Fertility tracking apps, which were initially marketed as tools to help women understand their reproductive health, have become instruments of surveillance. In states with strict abortion laws, data from these apps can be subpoenaed and used as evidence to prosecute women suspected of terminating pregnancies. Employers and insurers may also exploit this data to deny healthcare coverage or impose punitive measures. The erosion of digital privacy is emblematic of the broader culture of surveillance under Project 2025, where women's lives are treated as open books, subject to scrutiny by the state, employers, and even neighbors. This invasive monitoring transforms everyday decisions, whether to track a menstrual cycle, seek medical care, or confide in a friend, into potential liabilities.

The psychological toll of living under constant surveillance and scrutiny cannot be overstated. Women are forced to navigate a landscape where every choice carries the risk of judgment or punishment, creating a state of perpetual hyper-vigilance. The regime's policies foster a culture of shame and fear, where women internalize the blame for outcomes beyond their control. This erosion of self-trust is not incidental but a deliberate outcome of policies designed to render women passive, compliant, and disconnected from their sense of agency. The message is clear: a woman's body is not her own but belongs to the state, the community, and the cultural order upheld by Project 2025.

This control extends into personal relationships, where societal policing exacerbates existing power imbalances. Women in interracial, LGBTQ+, or otherwise nontraditional partnerships face heightened scrutiny, as their choices are seen as challenges to the regime's vision of acceptable unions. Even women in more traditional relationships are not immune; the regime's rhetoric emboldens some men to assert dominance, framing control over their partners as both a right and a duty. The pressure to conform to societal expectations forces many women into relationships that are neither safe nor fulfilling, perpetuating cycles of disempowerment and abuse. At the same time, the cultural emphasis on surveillance and judgment undermines the trust and solidarity necessary for healthy relationships, replacing mutual respect with fear and suspicion.

While legal mechanisms like travel restrictions and bounty laws form the backbone of Project 2025's assault on women's autonomy, the cultural and psychological strategies supporting these measures are just as pervasive and insidious. By embedding patriarchal norms into the social fabric, the regime ensures that the policing of women's bodies extends beyond the reach of legislation into the intimate spaces of daily life. Cultural expectations, societal judgment, and psychological manipulation become tools of control, creating an environment where women are not only watched but also expected to self-regulate in accordance with the regime's vision. This web of control reinforces isolation, suppresses resistance, and amplifies the regime's power.

Central to this cultural policing is the reinforcement of patriarchal ideals through societal messaging. The regime's rhetoric positions women's conformity to traditional roles as essential to maintaining moral order and societal stability. Women are told their highest calling is to be mothers and caregivers, and any deviation from this path is framed as selfish or unnatural. The language of "family values" serves as a Trojan horse for policies and cultural norms designed to limit women's opportunities and choices. Ambitious women who prioritize their careers are cast as neglectful; single women who delay or reject motherhood are labeled as incomplete. This messaging isn't passive; it's woven into media, education, and even public health campaigns, ensuring its omnipresence in women's lives.

Religious institutions are particularly powerful in propagating these messages, leveraging faith to uphold patriarchal systems. Evangelical leaders aligned with Project 2025 often preach submission and obedience as divine mandates for women, turning religious belief into a justification for control. These sermons frame women's autonomy as a threat to family and community, portraying resistance as sinful rebellion. This weaponization of faith silences dissent within religious communities and pressures women into accepting subjugation as a moral duty. Churches become not sanctuaries but battlegrounds, where women's roles are dictated and their choices scrutinized.

While cultural policing dictates how women should live, surveillance ensures compliance. Digital tools like fertility tracking apps, once celebrated for empowering women to manage their health, have been co-opted to enforce reproductive control. Employers and insurers increasingly demand access to this data, and in states with restrictive abortion laws, it can be used as evidence in legal proceedings. This weaponization of technology transforms seemingly benign activities, like tracking a menstrual cycle, into acts fraught with risk. Social media, too, becomes a tool of oppression, where women's posts are monitored for signs of dissent or nonconformity. Anti-abortion activists scour online platforms to identify and harass women seeking reproductive healthcare, eroding the sense of safety and community these spaces once offered.

This culture of surveillance is not limited to the digital realm. In communities aligned with Project 2025's ideology, neighbors, coworkers, and even family members are encouraged to report women who may be violating abortion laws or defying societal expectations. The normalization of citizen policing fosters a climate of fear and distrust, isolating women from potential allies. Clinics providing reproductive healthcare are surrounded by protestors who record license plates and follow patients, turning what should be a private medical decision into a public spectacle. Women are left to navigate a minefield where every action, seeking care, confiding in a friend, or even traveling out of state, could lead to judgment, harassment, or legal repercussions.

The psychological toll of this constant monitoring and judgment is profound. Living under surveillance forces women into a state of hyper-vigilance, where every decision must be calculated to minimize risk. This chronic stress wears down mental and emotional resilience, leaving women exhausted and disconnected from their sense of self. Over time, many internalize the shame and fear imposed by the regime, accepting blame for circumstances beyond their control. This internalization is not accidental; it is a deliberate outcome of policies designed to suppress dissent by undermining self-confidence and autonomy. Women begin to self-police, adjusting their behavior to avoid scrutiny and punishment, effectively doing the regime's work for it.

This erosion of autonomy extends into personal relationships, turning intimate spaces into sites of control. Women in interracial, LGBTQ+, or otherwise nontraditional relationships face heightened scrutiny, as their unions challenge the regime's narrow definitions of family and morality. These partnerships are often stigmatized or targeted, forcing women to navigate not only societal judgment but also legal and cultural barriers. Even within more traditional relationships, the regime's rhetoric reinforces unequal power dynamics, emboldening some men to exert control over their partners. Women may feel pressured to conform to their partners' expectations, sacrificing their own needs and desires to maintain harmony or avoid conflict. In this environment, leaving an unhealthy or abusive relationship becomes even more difficult, as societal pressure to conform outweighs concerns for personal safety.

Community dynamics are similarly affected. The regime's emphasis on conformity and surveillance undermines the trust and solidarity necessary for collective resistance. Women who might otherwise support one another are encouraged to compete or judge, reinforcing the isolation that makes the regime's policies so effective. This fracturing of community is intentional, as divided populations are easier to control. By turning neighbors into informants and friends into threats, the regime ensures that women remain isolated, unable to organize or advocate for change.

The core of Project 2025 is not merely a political agenda but a theological vision that seeks to reshape America into a Christian nationalist state. Its proponents aim to enforce a narrowly defined set of "biblical" principles as the law of the land, claiming moral authority while betraying the very ideals of justice, compassion, and equality that they purport to uphold. At the heart of this movement is a deep and deliberate hypocrisy: a demand for freedom that simultaneously seeks to deny others theirs, a call for moral purity that is blind to its own corruption, and a desire for control that betrays the foundational principles of democracy.

For women, the implications of this agenda are staggering. Under Project 2025, the Christian nationalist vision does not stop at rolling back reproductive rights; it stretches toward the wholesale subjugation of women, from restricting their roles in society to questioning their very right to participate in democratic governance. This movement is a chilling step toward a form of Christian theocracy, or what some have aptly termed "Christian Sharia law," imposed in the name of God and patriotism.

Protecting personal data is crucial when using women's health apps, as many have been found to mishandle sensitive information. To safeguard your privacy, consider the following apps and websites known for their strong data protection practices:

Clue
A menstrual cycle tracking app that adheres to strict European data privacy standards, ensuring user data is not shared with third parties.

Euki
Developed by Women Help Women, this app allows users to track reproductive health without collecting or storing personal data, enhancing privacy.

Drip
An open-source menstrual cycle tracker that emphasizes data privacy, allowing users to store data locally without third-party access.

Natural Cycles
A certified contraceptive app that uses basal body temperature to monitor fertility, committed to user data protection and privacy.

Spot On
Created by Planned Parenthood, this period and birth control tracker ensures user data is kept confidential and not shared with third parties.

Obsidian
A secure, encrypted note-taking app that can be used to privately document health information without data being stored on external servers.

ProtonMail
An encrypted email service that allows secure communication with healthcare providers, ensuring sensitive information remains confidential.

Signal
A messaging app offering end-to-end encryption, suitable for discussing personal health matters securely.

DuckDuckGo
A privacy-focused search engine that doesn't track user activity, useful for researching health information without leaving a data trail.

Tor Browser
Enables anonymous internet browsing, helping users access health information without being tracked.

Bonus Tips
Regularly review app privacy policies to ensure they align with your needs.
Avoid sharing sensitive health data on apps without clear privacy commitments.
Back up critical health information securely on devices you control, not just in cloud storage.
Use strong passwords and two-factor authentication for all accounts managing health-related data.

Checklist to Prepare for Policing of Women's Bodies

Learn Basic Self-Defense
Take self-defense classes to feel more confident navigating potentially unsafe situations.

Stay Informed
Keep up with changes in laws, local policies, and news affecting women's rights and healthcare.

Reclaim Control of Fertility Tracking
Use offline or manual tracking methods like calendars or paper charts to avoid digital surveillance.
Be cautious about sharing reproductive health details with healthcare providers in states with strict laws.

Understand Your Legal Rights
Familiarize yourself with local laws on reproductive health, dress codes, and workplace policies.
Know your rights during police or legal interactions, especially regarding health-related matters.

Build a Support Network

Connect with trusted friends, family, and advocacy groups who can offer support and share resources.

Join local women's organizations or mutual aid networks for collective action and safety planning.

Educate Yourself and Others

Learn about reproductive health, consent, and privacy issues to counteract misinformation.

Share knowledge within your community to empower others to navigate these challenges.

Create a Safe Environment at Home

Foster open, nonjudgmental discussions about body autonomy with family members.

Teach children and teens about consent and privacy in age-appropriate ways.

Develop Strategies for Navigating Public Spaces

Dress in ways that balance personal expression with an awareness of potential judgment or enforcement in your area.

Identify where you can go in your community if you are unsafe.

Prepare Financially

Save for potential emergencies related to healthcare access or legal challenges.

Keep funds available for travel if needed to access out-of-state healthcare or safe spaces.

Practice Self-Care and Resilience

Prioritize mental and physical health through mindfulness, exercise, and supportive relationships.

Seek therapy or counseling if the pressure of surveillance and societal judgment feels overwhelming.

Document and Report Injustices

Keep a record of any incidents of discrimination, harassment, or legal issues to use as evidence if needed.

Share stories responsibly to raise awareness and strengthen collective resistance.

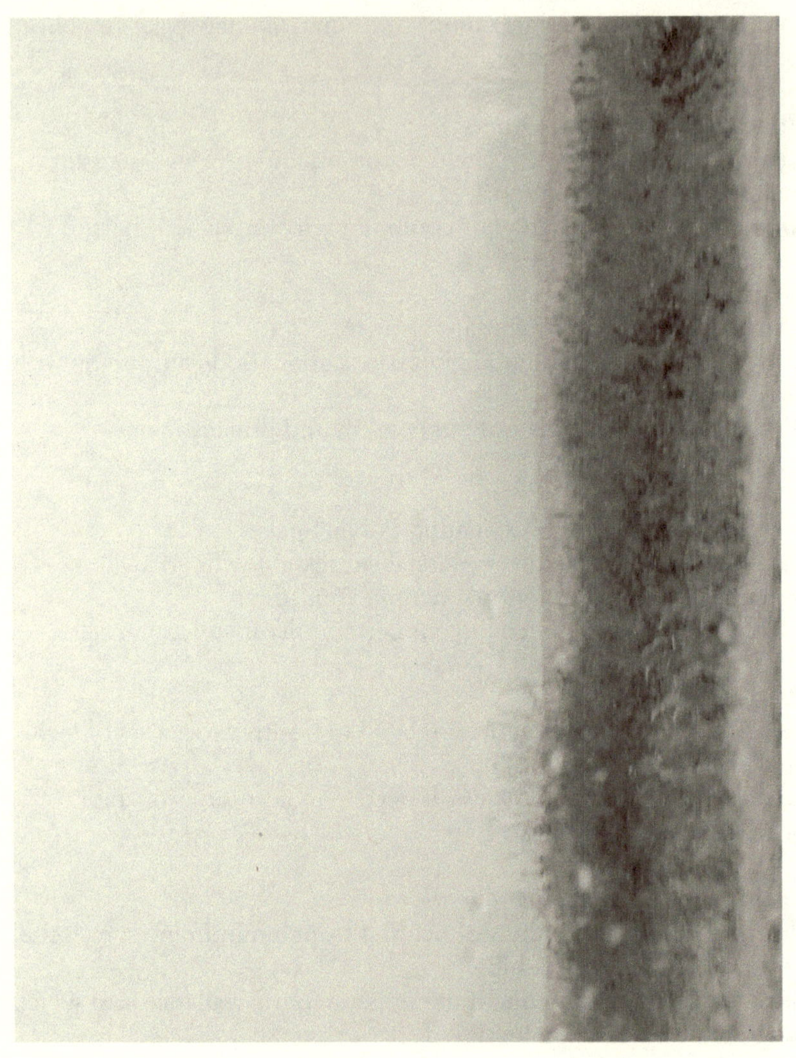

The Ten Plagues of Project 2025
9~The Collapse of Community Safety Nets

The deliberate dismantling of community safety nets under Project 2025 represents one of the most devastating attacks on collective resilience and equity. Services like libraries, shelters, and public health initiatives have long been lifelines for individuals and families, particularly for women, single mothers, and low-income communities. These institutions provided not only material support but also spaces for empowerment, education, and connection. Now, under the Reek regime's austerity measures and ideological agenda, these essential services are being defunded and dismantled, leaving communities to fend for themselves in an increasingly hostile and unequal society.

Libraries, once the quiet cornerstones of public education and civic life, are among the first casualties. These institutions, which offer far more than books, have been critical for providing free access to the internet, safe spaces for children, and resources for job seekers, students, and marginalized groups. For many, libraries were the only place to access knowledge without a price tag attached. Under Project 2025, however, libraries are rebranded as "inefficient" or "outdated," with their funding diverted to private initiatives or simply cut altogether. The loss is immeasurable: a hollowing out of intellectual resources and public space where women and families could feel safe and supported. For communities already struggling with inequity, this defunding removes one of the last remaining avenues for upward mobility and connection.

Shelters and crisis services, essential for those fleeing domestic violence or facing homelessness, have fared no better. The regime's policy of "self-reliance" is a thinly veiled attempt to shirk responsibility for the vulnerable, cutting budgets for shelters and programs that provided refuge and stability for countless women and families. The consequences are dire. Women escaping abusive relationships find themselves with no place to turn, forced to choose between staying in danger or facing homelessness. Shelters that remain open are overwhelmed, understaffed, and underfunded, leaving them ill-equipped to handle the growing demand. The regime's refusal to prioritize these services is not just a failure of governance, it is a calculated move to deepen inequality and entrench patriarchal control.

Public health initiatives, long the safety nets for communities lacking adequate healthcare, have also been eviscerated. Programs aimed at providing reproductive health services, mental health support, and preventive care are systematically dismantled under the guise of fiscal conservatism. Clinics close, outreach programs vanish, and women are left navigating an increasingly inaccessible healthcare landscape. Maternal mortality rates rise as prenatal care becomes harder to access, while preventable diseases resurge due to the collapse of vaccination programs and public awareness campaigns. The regime's defunding of public health isn't just short-sighted, it's a direct attack on the well-being of those who rely on these services to survive.

This collapse of safety nets is part of a broader ideological agenda. By eliminating public resources, the regime forces individuals to turn to private entities, religious organizations, or exploitative systems that often come with strings attached. For women and families, this means navigating systems that prioritize obedience over autonomy, charity over dignity. The goal is clear: to strip communities of their independence and force reliance on structures that reinforce the regime's values. In this context, the dismantling of safety nets is not just about saving money, it is about consolidating control.

Despite these challenges, communities are finding ways to resist and rebuild. Grassroots networks are emerging as an antidote to the regime's neglect, driven by the understanding that survival depends on mutual aid and collective action. These networks, often led by women, provide immediate support while laying the groundwork for long-term resilience. At their core is the idea that communities can and must take care of one another, creating systems of care that operate outside of the state's reach.

Building grassroots networks begins with identifying local needs and resources. This might mean mapping out who in the neighborhood has access to food, transportation, or skills that can be shared. For instance, someone with a garden might contribute fresh produce, while another neighbor offers childcare or transportation to medical appointments. These exchanges, while seemingly small, create a web of support that grows stronger with each connection. The power of grassroots networks lies in their ability to adapt to specific community needs, making them far more effective than one-size-fits-all solutions.

Food security is one area where grassroots efforts can make a tangible difference. Community gardens, food-sharing programs, and collective cooking initiatives are powerful tools for addressing hunger while fostering connection. Gardens can be planted in backyards, empty lots, or even on balconies, transforming underutilized spaces into sources of nourishment and hope. Food-sharing programs, where neighbors pool resources or distribute surplus food, ensure that no one goes hungry. These initiatives not only meet immediate needs but also challenge the regime's narrative of scarcity and competition.

Shelter and housing are another priority for grassroots networks. With shelters overwhelmed or nonexistent, communities are stepping in to provide temporary housing solutions. This might mean opening homes to families in crisis, creating safe sleeping spaces in community centers or religious institutions, or even forming cooperatives to pool resources for shared housing. These efforts, while imperfect, offer a lifeline for those who would otherwise be left behind. Long-term, grassroots networks can advocate for policies like rent control, tenant protections, and the development of affordable housing, pushing back against the systemic forces driving the housing crisis.

Public health, too, can be supported through local efforts. Community health initiatives, such as wellness workshops, mental health support groups, or mobile clinics, provide care in the absence of state-funded programs. Women with medical or counseling expertise can offer their skills on a volunteer or low-cost basis, ensuring that critical needs are met. Networks can also distribute health supplies, such as menstrual products or over-the-counter medications, reducing the burden on those who might otherwise go without.

Education, another critical safety net, is being reimagined by grassroots networks. With libraries closing and schools underfunded, communities are creating alternative spaces for learning. Book exchanges, tutoring programs, and skill-sharing workshops offer opportunities for children and adults to continue their education outside traditional institutions. These initiatives empower individuals to gain knowledge and skills that will serve them in a challenging environment, building both resilience and hope.

Turning neighborhoods into hubs of resistance requires creativity, collaboration, and a commitment to collective well-being. It begins with the simple act of reaching out, knocking on a neighbor's door, hosting a community meeting, or starting a conversation at the local park. These small actions can lead to the creation of networks that transform despair into action, showing that even in the absence of institutional support, communities have the power to care for one another.

The collapse of community safety nets is devastating, but it is not the end of the story. By building grassroots networks, reclaiming public spaces, and prioritizing collective care, women and families can resist the regime's agenda and create new systems of support. These efforts are not just about survival, they are about reclaiming agency and dignity in the face of systemic oppression. Together, we can build a future where safety nets are not just restored but reimagined to serve everyone, equally and equitably.

The second part of The Collapse of Community Safety Nets delves into the deeper implications of rebuilding these systems from the ground up, emphasizing the transformative power of grassroots resistance. While the Reek regime seeks to weaken the fabric of communities through the destruction of essential services, these acts of dismantling inadvertently reveal the strength and ingenuity of ordinary people. The collapse of state-supported safety nets forces neighborhoods, especially women-led initiatives, to reimagine what support, care, and resistance look like. This part explores how communities can turn collective struggles into opportunities for empowerment and solidarity.

The heart of rebuilding safety nets lies in fostering mutual trust and collaboration within communities. This starts with listening. Understanding the unique needs of your neighborhood, whether it's access to food, healthcare, transportation, or emotional support, creates a foundation for effective action. Trust-building involves transparency, inclusion, and respect for the diverse experiences and talents that community members bring to the table. Organizing events like potlucks, neighborhood cleanups, or town hall meetings can foster connections and establish a culture of cooperation. In a society designed to isolate and alienate, these gatherings become acts of quiet defiance, reminders that unity is the greatest strength against systemic neglect.

One of the most effective ways to resist the regime's erasure of public services is to reclaim and repurpose abandoned spaces. Vacant lots, closed libraries, or shuttered community centers can become hubs for grassroots action. Imagine a vacant lot transformed into a thriving garden, where families grow vegetables while teaching children about sustainability. Or a closed library converted into a learning center, offering free tutoring, workshops, and internet access. These spaces, reclaimed by and for the community, challenge the narrative that public resources are obsolete or unnecessary. They are physical manifestations of resistance, symbols of what can be built when people refuse to accept the regime's vision of scarcity.

Grassroots networks must also prioritize inclusivity, ensuring that no one is left behind. Women, single mothers, LGBTQ+ individuals, immigrants, and people with disabilities often bear the brunt of systemic failures. Creating safe, welcoming spaces for these groups is essential. For example, childcare cooperatives can allow single mothers to work or attend school without the crushing burden of unaffordable daycare. LGBTQ+ support groups can provide affirmation and advocacy in regions where their rights are under attack. These initiatives not only meet immediate needs but also empower marginalized voices, challenging the regime's attempts to erase them.

Education remains a cornerstone of resilience and resistance. With traditional systems failing, grassroots networks must step up to fill the void. This can include creating informal homeschooling collectives, where parents and volunteers share teaching responsibilities and resources. Libraries, whether physical or digital, can be rebuilt through book drives, donations, and open-source platforms. Skill-sharing workshops, where community members teach everything from basic literacy to advanced trades, foster self-sufficiency and mutual respect. By prioritizing education, communities equip themselves with the tools needed to challenge the regime's narrative and build a better future.

Economic empowerment is another critical element of grassroots resistance. As public services and job opportunities dwindle, communities can create alternative systems that prioritize equity and sustainability. Time banks, where neighbors exchange services like childcare, tutoring, or home repairs without money changing hands, are one example. Worker cooperatives, where employees collectively own and manage businesses, offer another model for economic stability. These initiatives challenge the exploitative practices of traditional systems while fostering a sense of ownership and agency among participants. For women, who are often excluded from economic power, these models provide a pathway to independence and leadership.

Healthcare, while one of the most challenging areas to address, is also one of the most vital. Communities can organize health fairs, where volunteer medical professionals provide free checkups, vaccinations, and health education. Peer support groups for mental health, addiction recovery, or chronic illness can offer a lifeline to those who feel abandoned by traditional systems. Women's health, in particular, requires focused attention. Grassroots networks can distribute contraception, menstrual products, and prenatal care resources while advocating for broader access to reproductive healthcare. These efforts, though small in scale, save lives and remind communities of their inherent worth.

Resistance also requires confronting the regime's attempts to undermine public discourse and solidarity. Misinformation, fearmongering, and propaganda are powerful tools for dividing communities. Grassroots networks must counter these forces by creating spaces for honest, informed dialogue. Community newspapers, social media groups, or even bulletin boards at local markets can disseminate accurate information, challenge harmful narratives, and amplify marginalized voices. Storytelling, through art, music, or writing, becomes a powerful tool for preserving history and inspiring action.

Ultimately, the collapse of safety nets under Project 2025 is not just a policy failure, it is an opportunity for communities to reclaim their power and redefine what care and support look like. Grassroots networks are not perfect, nor can they replace the scale and reach of state-supported systems. But they offer something more profound: a vision of society built on compassion, equity, and collective responsibility. These networks challenge the regime's narrative that survival is an individual struggle, replacing it with the truth that we are stronger together.

As these grassroots efforts grow, they serve as a blueprint for a more just and resilient society. They demonstrate that even in the face of systemic neglect and oppression, communities have the power to rebuild and reimagine. The Reek regime may have destroyed the safety nets, but it cannot destroy the spirit of those who refuse to give up. Together, we can weave new nets, stronger, more inclusive, and more enduring than ever before. This is not just survival; this is resistance. And in that resistance lies the seeds of a better future.

Short Story: *Once Upon a Time in the Ashes*

Once upon a time, everything felt awful and hopeless. The roads were crumbling, the libraries were shuttered, and people whispered about how the government cared more for billionaires than for families scraping to survive. It seemed as though the powerful had won, locking the world into a dark age of greed and control. But in a small, forgotten town, something remarkable began to stir.

It started with a garden. A woman named Ruth, tired of waiting for help that never came, turned an abandoned lot into a place of hope. She planted vegetables, invited her neighbors, and soon the garden became a gathering spot for the community. People who hadn't spoken in years began to share seeds, stories, and meals. It wasn't much, but it was a start.

The garden inspired others. A teacher named Luis started a free library on his porch, filling it with books salvaged from the shuttered town library. A mechanic named Angie began offering free classes on fixing cars and bicycles, helping people regain mobility without relying on costly services. Parents organized a childcare co-op so they could work or attend school without paying more than they earned.

In time, the town's small victories began to grow into something larger. Neighbors formed councils to make decisions together, replacing the absentee officials who had long ignored their needs. They created community funds to help with medical emergencies and built solar panels to power their homes. They didn't wait for permission or funding, they reclaimed what was theirs.

Word spread. Other towns, inspired by the small acts of defiance and resilience, began to follow suit. Networks of cooperation stretched across counties and states, forming a web of communities that prioritized care over profit, equity over exploitation. What had once been isolated acts of survival became a movement.

The oligarchs and their enforcers sneered at first, calling it insignificant. But they underestimated the power of people who had nothing left to lose and everything to gain. The communities grew stronger, more connected, and more determined. They created their own systems, schools, clinics, and marketplaces, outside the reach of corrupt officials. They turned their neighborhoods into sanctuaries of resistance and hope.

The fascistic oligarchs tried to crush the movement, but they were too late. The people had tasted self-governance, and they refused to give it up. What began as a garden in a forgotten town became the foundation of a nation reclaimed, rebuilt, and reimagined. The future wasn't in the hands of the few anymore, it belonged to everyone.

And so, what once seemed hopeless became a story of transformation. The seeds of despair grew into fields of possibility, proving that even in the darkest times, hope and courage can light the way.

Checklist to Prepare for the Collapse of Community Safety Nets

Build Local Relationships

Get to know your neighbors and establish trust. Strong relationships are the foundation of mutual aid and community resilience.

Identify Community Resources

Map out existing resources like community centers, libraries, food banks, or clinics. Understand what is available and where gaps exist.

Learn Basic Survival Skills

Acquire skills such as gardening, first aid, food preservation, and basic repairs. These can be invaluable in a resource-limited environment.

Stock Essential Supplies
Create a personal emergency kit with non-perishable food, water, medications, and other necessities. Encourage others in your community to do the same.

Organize Mutual Aid Networks
Join or start a local mutual aid group to pool resources, share skills, and provide support for neighbors in need.

Create Shared Spaces
Identify unused or underutilized spaces that can be repurposed as community hubs for education, resource distribution, or safe gatherings.

Prioritize Education
Organize community-led tutoring, skill-sharing workshops, or informal classes to replace lost educational resources like libraries and after-school programs.

Advocate for Local Solutions
Push for policies like rent control, tenant protections, and funding for local services. Organize community campaigns to hold local officials accountable.

Develop Communication Networks
Set up local communication channels, such as group chats or bulletin boards, to quickly share information, needs, and resources within the community.

Foster Emotional and Mental Resilience
Create support groups or safe spaces where neighbors can share their experiences and offer encouragement. Building emotional strength is key to collective survival.

The Ten Plagues of Project 2025
10~Women in the Crosshairs of Fascism

The rise of Project 2025 thrusts women into an unprecedented struggle for autonomy and dignity. Far from relics of the past, archaic gender roles, forced marriages, and purity culture are wielded as deliberate tools of control. The Reek regime has resurrected an extreme vision of traditional gender roles, not as a nostalgic return to simpler times but as a strategic mechanism to maintain rigid hierarchies. Women are cast as submissive caretakers, expected to carry the moral and emotional weight of their families while being denied agency, ambition, or respect. This is not a passive suggestion, it is enforced through policies, propaganda, and societal judgment. Career aspirations are vilified as distractions from a woman's "true purpose," while men are celebrated as protectors and providers, reinforcing dependency and perpetuating inequality. This system doesn't just thrive on inequality; it demands it, ensuring that women's labor is exploited without recognition and that their existence is tethered to the roles assigned by the regime.

Forced marriages, long thought to belong to history or far-off dystopias, have returned as grim realities. The regime manipulates legal frameworks to ensure women are bound to men, where marriage becomes less about partnership and more about ownership. Women in abusive relationships find that the options to escape have been erased, with divorce made nearly impossible and legal protections for survivors dismantled. Community and religious leaders, empowered by the regime's policies, pressure women into unions under the guise of tradition and stability, framing such sacrifices as necessary for the "greater good." For many women, marriage becomes a prison, ensuring obedience and reinforcing the patriarchal structures that benefit the regime. This commodification of women's lives not only denies them freedom but ensures that they remain tools for sustaining a system that thrives on their subjugation.

Purity culture, simmering in the undercurrents of conservative ideologies, has been elevated to state doctrine. Girls are indoctrinated early, taught that their worth is tied to their sexual purity and adherence to restrictive gender norms. Abstinence-only education, strict dress codes, and public shaming campaigns reinforce the idea that women's bodies are inherently sinful unless controlled by male authority. The consequences are far-reaching, creating a culture of fear and self-loathing where women feel responsible not only for their actions but also for the behavior of the men around them. This narrative isolates women, encouraging them to police themselves and each other while perpetuating cycles of shame and subjugation. By reducing women to symbols of purity, the regime ensures that their individuality, ambition, and autonomy are erased.

In this openly hostile society, even acts of compassion and care work become radical. Women who provide shelter for those fleeing forced marriages or abusive relationships, who offer counseling to survivors of violence, or who educate girls about their rights are not simply supporting others, they are committing acts of rebellion. Care work, often dismissed as invisible or insignificant, becomes revolutionary in a system that seeks to erode community and solidarity. By fostering resilience and connection, these acts directly challenge the regime's attempts to isolate and dehumanize women. In this way, compassion is transformed into a form of resistance, reminding women of their shared strength and humanity.

To navigate this dangerous terrain, women must adopt strategies that prioritize safety, solidarity, and defiance. Building informal support networks is essential, creating lifelines for women to escape dangerous situations or access critical resources. These networks must operate with discretion, using encrypted communication and trusted contacts to avoid detection. They offer not only material support but also a sense of hope and connection in a world designed to break it. Education, too, becomes a critical tool of resistance. While formal systems may fail women, informal learning spaces can fill the gap, teaching women and girls about their rights, their history, and their power. Sharing practical skills, such as financial literacy, first aid, and self-defense, equips women to protect themselves and their families while planting seeds of long-term resilience.

Art and storytelling also play a vital role in this fight. Women's voices, long silenced, find power in creative expression. Writing, painting, music, and performance become tools for documenting experiences, challenging narratives, and inspiring action. Public art projects, underground publications, or shared songs create a sense of shared purpose and remind women that their stories matter. These acts of creation are not just personal, they are political, asserting that women's lives have value and that their perspectives are worth hearing. They challenge the regime's attempts to erase individuality and foster solidarity among women who might otherwise feel alone in their struggles.

Ultimately, the fight against the regime's oppression of women requires both individual resilience and collective action. The stakes are high, but history has shown that women are at their strongest when they come together to fight for justice. By refusing to conform to imposed roles, by building networks of care and resistance, and by reclaiming their voices, women can push back against the forces that seek to control them. In a world that views them as second-class citizens, every act of defiance is a step toward liberation and a reminder that the future is still worth fighting for. This is not just a battle for survival, it is a battle for the right to exist fully, freely, and unapologetically.

The second half of Women in the Crosshairs of Fascism explores the strategies women are developing to fight back against a system that seeks to erase their autonomy and humanity. While the Reek regime aims to reduce women to roles of subservience and compliance, these oppressive tactics inadvertently ignite new forms of resistance. Women, often underestimated by those in power, are reclaiming spaces, rewriting narratives, and finding innovative ways to challenge a regime that thrives on fear and division.

One of the most powerful tools for resistance is the reclamation of public and private spaces. Women are turning kitchens, churches, and even abandoned buildings into sanctuaries where they can gather, strategize, and provide care for one another. These spaces serve as hubs for knowledge-sharing, from teaching self-defense to organizing safe passage for women fleeing dangerous situations. The regime's surveillance and puritanical policies attempt to suppress such gatherings, but the resilience of women ensures that these sanctuaries persist. Often, the act of simply occupying space and creating community in defiance of the regime becomes a form of protest, a bold statement that their lives and connections cannot be controlled.

Technology, while often weaponized against women through surveillance and doxxing, is also being used to subvert the regime's control. Encrypted messaging apps and digital privacy tools allow women to communicate, organize, and share information safely. Online platforms become spaces for solidarity, where women share their stories, amplify each other's voices, and coordinate resistance efforts across geographical boundaries. Women are also using social media to highlight injustices and spread awareness of their plight, despite the risks of backlash and censorship. This digital resistance is not just about survival, it's about reclaiming visibility and agency in a world that seeks to render them invisible.

Cultural resistance, particularly through art, is another potent weapon against the regime. Women are creating subversive works that critique the regime's policies and celebrate their defiance. Underground zines, guerrilla art installations, and anonymous performances become tools for exposing the absurdity and cruelty of the Reek regime. These creations inspire hope and action, reminding women that they are not alone in their struggles. More importantly, art creates a sense of collective identity, uniting women across different backgrounds and experiences in their shared resistance.

Relationships, too, become acts of defiance in this environment. Women are forming alliances that transcend traditional boundaries, building coalitions with other marginalized groups to resist the regime's oppression. Solidarity between women of different races, classes, and orientations challenges the divisive tactics of the regime. These coalitions are powerful not just for their ability to coordinate action but also for their ability to foster understanding and shared purpose. In many cases, the act of simply standing together in the face of adversity becomes a revolutionary statement.

At the individual level, women are redefining what strength looks like in a hostile society. For some, this means quiet acts of rebellion, like mentoring younger women, sharing banned books, or offering a listening ear to those in need. For others, it means bold, public defiance, speaking out at rallies, challenging discriminatory policies in court, or documenting abuses for the world to see. Both forms of resistance are equally valid and necessary, demonstrating that there is no single way to fight back. Each woman's act of courage, no matter how small, contributes to a larger movement that chips away at the regime's power.

Even in the face of such profound hostility, women are finding ways to protect and nurture their mental and emotional well-being. Support groups, whether in-person or online, provide safe spaces where women can share their fears, frustrations, and triumphs without judgment. These groups are vital not just for survival but for sustaining the hope and determination needed to keep resisting. Practices like journaling, meditation, and creating art also offer outlets for processing the trauma inflicted by the regime, allowing women to reclaim a sense of control over their narratives and lives.

Perhaps the most remarkable aspect of this resistance is its unyielding optimism. Women are not just fighting for survival, they are fighting for a better future, one where equality and autonomy are no longer radical ideas but basic human rights. This vision of the future drives their efforts, giving them the strength to endure setbacks and the courage to continue despite the odds. It's a future they may not live to see, but one they are determined to create for their daughters, their communities, and generations yet to come.

In a society that has placed them in the crosshairs, women are proving that their resilience, creativity, and solidarity are more powerful than the forces arrayed against them. By reclaiming their spaces, their voices, and their futures, they are not just surviving, they are building a foundation for liberation. The Reek regime may believe it has the power to silence women, but in reality, it has only amplified their determination to fight for a world where they are no longer targets but equals. This is their resistance, their revolution, and their story. It is a story of courage, defiance, and the unshakable belief that even in the darkest times, a brighter future can be forged.

Final Checklist to Prepare for Women in the Crosshairs of Fascism

Create an Emergency Plan

Develop a plan for quick escapes from dangerous situations, including safe destinations, emergency contacts, and essential supplies.

Identify trusted allies who can provide temporary shelter or transportation.

Gather Critical Documents

Secure copies of identification, birth certificates, marriage and divorce documents, medical records, and financial information.

Keep these in a waterproof, portable bag or encrypt them digitally for secure access.

Learn Encryption and Privacy Tools

Use apps like Signal for encrypted communication and Tor for anonymous browsing.

Familiarize yourself with secure methods for storing and sharing sensitive information.

Strengthen Financial Independence

Open a separate bank account if possible and save small amounts regularly for emergencies.

Learn financial literacy basics, including budgeting and protecting assets from potential control by others.

Understand and Protect Your Legal Rights

Research local laws regarding marriage, custody, and domestic violence protections.

Keep contact information for legal aid organizations and attorneys who specialize in women's rights.

Build a Personal Support Network

Form alliances with trusted friends, family, or community members who can offer practical and emotional support.

Join local or online women's groups for shared knowledge and resources.

Stockpile Health and Personal Supplies

Collect essential health items, such as menstrual products, contraceptives, vitamins, and medications.

Include non-perishable food, water, first-aid kits, and portable power sources in your emergency stockpile.

Learn Basic Self-Defense

Take classes or watch tutorials on self-defense techniques to increase your confidence and safety.

Carry tools like whistles, pepper spray (if legal in your area), or personal alarms.

Develop Practical Skills

Acquire skills like sewing, food preservation, basic repairs, and gardening to reduce dependence on external systems.

Learn how to navigate bureaucratic systems effectively to access the remaining resources available.

Foster Emotional Resilience

Engage in practices like journaling, meditation, or art to manage stress and process trauma.

Seek therapy or join support groups to maintain mental health in difficult times.

Establish Safe Communication Channels

Use code words or signals with trusted contacts for discreet communication.

Avoid sharing sensitive information on platforms known for weak privacy protections.

Diversify and Document Your Knowledge

Create or contribute to underground networks that share banned books, educational materials, or historical records.

Document your own experiences to preserve truth and inspire future resistance.

Prepare for Community Advocacy

Stay informed about local issues affecting women and participate in campaigns to protect rights.

Develop skills for organizing protests, writing petitions, or speaking at public forums.

Teach the Next Generation

Educate children about equality, consent, and critical thinking to counteract indoctrination efforts.

Model resilience and defiance to inspire their confidence and courage.

Plan for Long-Term Challenges
Create a roadmap for education or career goals that align with building independence and security.
Stay adaptable, updating plans as laws or circumstances change.

Monitor Social and Political Changes
Keep track of evolving policies and public sentiments that impact women's rights.
Build alliances across communities to amplify resistance against oppressive systems.

Stay Physically Strong
Prioritize physical health through exercise, balanced nutrition, and regular checkups when possible.
Strengthen your endurance and mobility to prepare for potential challenges.

Protect and Amplify Your Voice
Use writing, art, or public speaking to share your perspective and challenge oppressive narratives.
Connect with journalists or advocacy organizations that amplify women's stories.

Support Others in Crisis
Offer time, resources, or emotional support to women in your network who are facing immediate threats.
Establish a community fund or resource pool to assist those in need.

Reclaim Joy and Creativity
Engage in activities that bring happiness and meaning, reminding yourself of the humanity the regime seeks to deny.
Celebrate small victories and moments of connection to sustain hope and motivation.

This comprehensive checklist ensures readiness for navigating a hostile environment while building strength, resilience, and solidarity for the road ahead. Every preparation, no matter how small, contributes to individual empowerment and collective resistance.

Visionary Fable: *The Land of Solara*

In a far-off time, nestled beyond the reach of greed's shadow, there was a land called Solara, where the pulse of life was shaped by compassion, empathy, and a quiet power that bound all together. The women of Solara governed with gentle wisdom, their leadership rooted not in conquest but in care. They sang to the forests to coax new growth, whispered to rivers to keep them clear, and spoke softly to their people, weaving peace into every thread of life.
In this world, there were no hierarchies of abuse, no systemic forces to gnaw at the soul. Kindness flourished as naturally as the morning sun. Justice was not blind but watchful, cradled in the hands of those who cherished fairness as a mother cherishes her child. Wealth was measured not in gold but in the laughter of children, the bloom of wildflowers, and the enduring warmth of shared meals. The land breathed a harmony that the world had once forgotten.

But the peace of Solara had not come without sacrifice. It was said that, long ago, the land had been plagued by the Furies of Self, cruel phantoms of greed and dominance. These wraiths whispered to the hearts of the vulnerable, urging them to hoard and hurt, to bend others to their will. The Furies fed on chaos, and for a time, they thrived, leaving Solara on the brink of ruin. But the women of the land, steadfast and united, did not wield weapons to fight them. Instead, they confronted the phantoms with unyielding compassion, turning venom into ash through acts of profound grace. They offered not submission but understanding, not destruction but forgiveness, and the Furies, starved of their power, dissolved into the earth.

Now, only one rule bound the land: the Circle of Reflection. Every deed, word, and thought passed through its silent judgment, would this action heal or harm? And so, the people of Solara lived without trauma, for they carried no burden that was not shared and inflicted no wound they could not bear themselves. It was not perfection, for perfection is a myth even in dreams, but it was enough, a life built on the power of care, where humanity had finally learned not to dominate but to nurture the world and one another.

Surviving/Thriving in the Post America Hellscape
11~DIY Reproductive Health

The battle for reproductive rights under Project 2025 has forced women to take control of their own health in ways that are both empowering and perilous. As access to safe, legal care becomes increasingly restricted, the burden of maintaining autonomy falls squarely on the shoulders of individuals and communities. Women must become their own advocates, researchers, and, at times, caregivers, navigating a labyrinth of legal, social, and medical obstacles. DIY reproductive health is not a choice born of convenience, it is a necessity born of survival in a system designed to deny women control over their bodies.

The first step in reclaiming reproductive autonomy is preparation. Stockpiling essential supplies is crucial, particularly in a landscape where access to birth control and other reproductive health tools is rapidly shrinking. Contraceptives such as condoms, emergency contraception (like Plan B), and hormonal birth control pills are vital resources to secure now, while they are still available. Long-term methods, such as IUDs or implants, are worth considering for those who can access them before restrictions tighten further. In addition to contraception, supplies like pregnancy tests, ovulation trackers, and menstrual products should be prioritized. These items not only aid in family planning but also serve as tools for monitoring reproductive health in the absence of professional care.

For those living in areas where access to contraception has already been curtailed, over-the-counter alternatives and herbal remedies can serve as stopgap measures, though they are far from ideal. Research into natural contraceptive methods, such as tracking basal body temperature or cervical mucus, can offer some control but requires precision and consistency. Herbal supplements like wild yam or pennyroyal have historically been used for birth control, but these options must be approached with caution and thorough research to ensure safety and efficacy. Women in this position must balance the risk of ineffective methods with the danger of relying on an unregulated underground network for supplies.

Accessing underground reproductive health services is an act of quiet rebellion that demands discretion and trust. In many regions, networks of individuals and organizations are stepping in where the system has failed, offering contraception, pregnancy support, and even abortion care in secret. These networks often operate under layers of anonymity, communicating through encrypted channels and word-of-mouth referrals. For those seeking these services, building relationships within trusted communities is essential. The underground thrives on mutual aid, but it is also vulnerable to infiltration and exploitation, making vigilance and caution paramount.

Knowledge is another indispensable tool in the DIY reproductive health arsenal. Women must arm themselves with an understanding of their own bodies, the medical options available to them, and the risks associated with each choice. Books on reproductive health, such as *Our Bodies, Ourselves*, offer foundational knowledge, while online resources and community workshops provide practical guidance. Learning how to administer basic care, from addressing common gynecological issues to managing early pregnancy symptoms, empowers women to act with confidence in the absence of professional support. For those facing unwanted pregnancies, understanding the options available, both legal and otherwise, is critical. Misoprostol, a medication used to induce abortion, has become a lifeline for many, but it requires precise dosing and access to medical guidance, even if through underground sources.

In this environment, discretion is as vital as knowledge. Women must learn how to navigate a surveillance-heavy society while seeking care. This means avoiding digital trails when searching for reproductive health information or purchasing supplies. Use secure browsers like Tor or privacy-focused search engines like DuckDuckGo to minimize tracking. Avoid discussing sensitive topics on platforms that store or share user data, and use encrypted messaging apps like Signal to communicate with trusted contacts. For physical interactions, discretion can mean choosing safe meeting places, relying on trusted intermediaries, or even creating plausible cover stories to avoid suspicion.

Despite the oppressive landscape, the resilience and ingenuity of women continue to shine through. Communities are pooling resources to create safe spaces for reproductive care, sharing supplies, and supporting one another in the face of shared adversity. Underground clinics, mutual aid funds, and even traveling healthcare providers are emerging as lifelines for those most at risk. These efforts are not without danger, but they reflect the unyielding spirit of women who refuse to relinquish control over their bodies and their futures.

DIY reproductive health is not an ideal solution. It carries risks, uncertainties, and the weight of navigating a system that has turned personal autonomy into an act of defiance. But it also represents a profound testament to the strength and solidarity of women. In a world that seeks to strip them of agency, they are finding ways to reclaim it, through preparation, education, and an unwavering commitment to one another. This fight is not just for survival; it is for the right to exist fully, freely, and with dignity. In the absence of a just system, women are building their own.

The second half of DIY Reproductive Health focuses on navigating the complexities of underground services and community-based solutions while minimizing risks and amplifying resilience. As Project 2025 tightens its grip, the ability to access safe reproductive care often hinges on creativity, resourcefulness, and the quiet defiance of oppressive systems. While the stakes are high, the collective ingenuity of women and their allies offers pathways to empowerment and survival.

Accessing underground reproductive health services requires a delicate balance of trust and caution. These networks often operate in the shadows, using encrypted communication tools, secret meeting locations, and pseudonyms to protect both providers and seekers. For those in need, the first step is identifying trusted entry points. Community organizers, mutual aid networks, or online forums can serve as bridges to these clandestine resources. However, navigating these spaces demands discretion. Women must verify sources carefully, avoiding scams or opportunistic actors who exploit vulnerability for profit or gain.

The art of discretion extends to every aspect of interacting with underground networks. Using cash instead of traceable electronic payments for supplies or services is a key strategy. When meeting contacts, women are advised to choose neutral, public locations and bring a trusted companion when possible. Phones or devices used to coordinate care should have location services disabled, and sensitive information should be deleted after use. This level of vigilance may feel invasive, but in a society where reproductive choices are criminalized, it is a necessary safeguard.

For those organizing within their communities, creating secure, decentralized systems is critical. Small, independent cells of volunteers can share resources and knowledge without compromising the entire network. Training sessions on how to administer medication, respond to complications, or offer emotional support are invaluable, ensuring that care extends beyond the initial act. Additionally, women with medical expertise can provide essential guidance, offering their skills discreetly while mentoring others to expand the community's capacity for care.

Stockpiling supplies for collective use is another practical step. Community resource hubs, whether physical or virtual, can distribute essential items like pregnancy tests, contraceptives, and safe abortion kits. These hubs often operate through mutual aid donations or crowd-sourced funding, ensuring that access is not limited by financial constraints. For women unable to participate directly in these networks, contributing supplies or funds to trusted groups is a way to support the cause from the periphery.

Education remains a cornerstone of the DIY reproductive health movement. Beyond individual learning, communities benefit from shared workshops and resource guides that demystify medical procedures, legal risks, and alternative options. Hosting regular discussions or classes on topics like herbal remedies, fertility tracking, or managing miscarriage ensures that knowledge is both accessible and shared widely. Women who become well-versed in these areas can act as community health leaders, bridging the gap left by inaccessible healthcare systems.

Self-advocacy is equally important in this hostile landscape. Women must understand how to navigate interactions with healthcare providers, especially in areas where reporting requirements or anti-abortion laws put patients at risk. Knowing what questions to ask, what rights to assert, and what information to withhold can mean the difference between receiving care and facing legal consequences. Role-playing scenarios with trusted allies can build confidence and prepare women for challenging situations.

Building emotional resilience is critical, especially in the face of systemic hostility. The psychological toll of navigating underground care, coupled with societal judgment, can be overwhelming. Peer support groups provide safe spaces for sharing experiences, offering encouragement, and processing trauma. These groups not only foster connection but also remind women that they are not alone in their struggles. Collective care is a radical act in a world that seeks to isolate and silence them.

Despite the regime's efforts to dismantle reproductive rights, women's defiance ensures that care continues. Underground networks, mutual aid groups, and informal educators are creating a parallel system that thrives on solidarity and innovation. The risks are undeniable, but so too is the power of collective action. Every act of resistance, whether it's helping a neighbor access contraception, sharing knowledge, or speaking out, strengthens the movement and chips away at the regime's control.

DIY reproductive health is a testament to the resilience of women in the face of oppression. While the system may fail them, their ingenuity and solidarity create new paths forward. This movement is not about returning to the way things were, it is about building something better. By reclaiming their autonomy, women are not just surviving, they are laying the foundation for a future where reproductive care is a right, not a privilege. In this fight, every small act matters, and every victory, no matter how small, moves the world closer to justice.

Surviving/Thriving in the Post America Hellscape 12~Building Financial Independence

In a world increasingly tilted toward the wealthy and powerful, financial independence becomes not just a goal but a form of survival. Under Project 2025, traditional jobs are less secure, wages fail to keep pace with inflation, and the systems meant to support working families have been gutted. For women, who are disproportionately affected by these economic pressures, the path to independence is littered with obstacles. Yet, even in a predatory system, resilience and resourcefulness can carve out spaces of autonomy. Saving, earning, and surviving in such an environment requires both strategic planning and a willingness to think beyond traditional economic models.

The first step to financial independence is understanding the landscape and creating a realistic plan to navigate it. For many, this begins with budgeting, a skill often undervalued yet crucial for maintaining control over one's finances. The key is to identify needs versus wants, tracking every expense to understand where money goes and where it can be saved. In a predatory economy, even small changes, like cutting unnecessary subscriptions or bulk buying essentials, can make a significant difference. Budgeting apps and spreadsheets can help organize this process, but pen and paper work just as well for those who prefer analog methods. The goal isn't just to cut costs but to reclaim agency over financial decisions in a system designed to erode it.

Saving is another cornerstone of financial independence, though it often feels impossible in a society where wages stagnate and costs soar. The first priority is building an emergency fund, even if it means starting small. A single month's worth of expenses saved can act as a critical buffer against sudden job loss, medical emergencies, or unexpected expenses. Creative strategies like rounding up every purchase to the nearest dollar and saving the difference or automating small transfers into a savings account can help build this safety net over time. Women must also protect their savings from potential exploitation, whether by controlling their own bank accounts or using discreet financial tools that prevent outside access.

Earning becomes a creative act of defiance when traditional jobs fail to provide stability. Side hustles, long dismissed as temporary solutions, have become lifelines for many. The key to a successful side hustle lies in identifying personal skills and resources that can be monetized. For some, this might mean selling handmade goods or offering freelance services online. For others, it could involve tapping into local needs, such as tutoring, pet care, or home repairs. Platforms like Etsy, Fiverr, or TaskRabbit offer opportunities to reach broader audiences, but women should also consider grassroots efforts, such as word-of-mouth advertising within their communities. The ultimate goal is to diversify income streams, reducing dependence on a single, unstable source of income.

In addition to side hustles, bartering and trade are gaining traction as alternative economic models. These systems bypass the need for cash altogether, relying instead on the exchange of goods and services. A woman who can sew might trade her skills for childcare, while another who grows vegetables might exchange them for home repairs. These informal networks foster community resilience and provide financial relief, particularly in regions where cash flow is tight. While bartering may not replace traditional income, it can significantly reduce expenses and create a sense of solidarity among participants.

Mutual aid networks are another crucial tool for financial independence, particularly in the absence of state support. These networks operate on the principle that everyone has something to contribute, whether it's money, time, or skills. Women who participate in mutual aid benefit not only from shared resources but also from the sense of security that comes from collective care. These networks often include emergency funds, food banks, or cooperative businesses, offering immediate support while building long-term stability. Unlike traditional charities, mutual aid is rooted in reciprocity and empowerment, ensuring that participants are both givers and receivers.

Building financial independence also requires a focus on skills development. Women must invest in learning that increases their earning potential, whether through formal education, online courses, or hands-on experience. Digital literacy, in particular, is increasingly critical as remote work and online business opportunities expand. Even basic computer skills can open doors to freelance writing, virtual assistance, or other flexible jobs. For those with access to community colleges or vocational programs, certifications in fields like healthcare, technology, or skilled trades offer pathways to higher wages and greater job security.

Another important consideration is debt management. In a predatory system, debt is both a tool and a trap, and women must navigate it carefully. Paying down high-interest debts, such as credit cards or payday loans, should be a priority, as these can quickly spiral out of control. At the same time, strategic use of low-interest loans or credit can provide opportunities for growth, such as starting a small business or pursuing further education. The key is to approach debt with caution and a clear plan, avoiding unnecessary risks while leveraging opportunities for advancement.

Finally, financial independence is not just about individual survival, it's about fostering collective strength. Women who achieve even small victories in building their financial independence can share their knowledge and resources with others, creating a ripple effect of empowerment. Workshops on budgeting, group savings programs, or mentorship initiatives can amplify these efforts, ensuring that no one is left behind. The predatory system thrives on isolation and competition, but women can counteract this by building networks of support and solidarity.

In a world designed to keep them economically dependent, women are finding ways to reclaim their power. Through careful planning, creative earning, and collective care, financial independence becomes not just a means of survival but a tool for resistance. It is a way to push back against a system that seeks to exploit and control, proving that even in the harshest conditions, women can thrive. This is not just about making ends meet, it is about building a foundation for autonomy, dignity, and hope. The path may be challenging, but every step taken is a step toward a future where women are no longer beholden to systems that fail them. Instead, they stand strong, with their financial destiny firmly in their own hands.

The second half of *Building Financial Independence* focuses on advanced strategies for securing economic autonomy in a system designed to exploit vulnerability. It's not enough to simply survive in a predatory economic environment, women must learn to thrive by outsmarting the structures meant to keep them dependent. This requires long-term planning, creative problem-solving, and a commitment to leveraging collective power.

Long-term financial security starts with investing in assets that build wealth over time. For some women, this might mean purchasing property, even in small or shared forms, to establish stability and equity. Cooperative housing models, where ownership and costs are shared among multiple families or individuals, can be a viable option when traditional homeownership feels out of reach. For others, starting a micro-business that can grow steadily with minimal overhead, such as an online shop or consultancy, provides a way to build income streams that are independent of external employers. While the regime's economic policies may favor corporations and the wealthy, small-scale entrepreneurship offers women a means to carve out their own space in the market.

Investing in personal and professional development is equally important. In a system where traditional opportunities may be limited, women must take proactive steps to ensure their skills remain relevant and competitive. Online platforms like Coursera, Udemy, and LinkedIn Learning offer affordable courses in high-demand areas like coding, graphic design, and project management. Local libraries, while they still exist, may also provide access to free workshops or training programs. Women should seek out mentors or join professional networks to gain insights into their chosen fields, fostering connections that can open doors to new opportunities.

For women juggling multiple responsibilities, time becomes as critical a resource as money. Developing systems to manage time efficiently, whether through scheduling apps, shared calendars, or simple prioritization techniques, can free up bandwidth to focus on earning or skill-building. Delegating tasks where possible, whether through childcare cooperatives or shared domestic responsibilities, allows women to redirect their energy toward financial goals. This is not a luxury; it is a necessary step in reclaiming agency over one's life.

Building financial independence also requires navigating systemic barriers with intention and resilience. Women must be prepared to advocate for themselves in workplaces that often undervalue their contributions. Negotiating salaries, demanding fair treatment, and pursuing promotions with confidence are acts of defiance against the wage gap and systemic sexism. For those in hostile or stagnant work environments, exploring alternative career paths or industries can provide an escape from oppressive systems. Entrepreneurship, freelancing, or transitioning to remote work are increasingly viable options for those seeking autonomy and flexibility.

Mutual aid networks remain a critical lifeline, especially for women facing systemic oppression. These networks go beyond immediate support, fostering long-term economic resilience by creating cooperative businesses, pooled savings funds, and resource-sharing platforms. Women who participate in mutual aid gain not only financial relief but also a sense of empowerment through collective action. These networks often extend beyond economics, becoming spaces for solidarity, education, and resistance. By sharing tools, knowledge, and opportunities, mutual aid transforms individual struggles into shared victories.

To secure long-term financial independence, women must also engage in wealth-building strategies, even on a small scale. This might involve starting a retirement fund through low-cost investment apps, purchasing government bonds, or learning the basics of stock market investing. While these options may seem inaccessible to those with limited means, starting small, by investing even $5 a month, can have a compounding effect over time. Financial literacy programs, whether online or community-based, can demystify these processes and empower women to take control of their financial futures.

Women must also remain vigilant against predatory practices designed to exploit their economic vulnerabilities. Payday loans, high-interest credit cards, and exploitative financial products often target those in desperate circumstances. Understanding these risks and seeking alternative solutions, such as community credit unions, peer-to-peer lending, or negotiating payment plans with creditors, can prevent women from falling into deeper financial traps. Advocacy groups and legal aid organizations can provide guidance for navigating these situations, ensuring that women are not left to face these challenges alone.

Finally, fostering a mindset of financial resilience is key. Women must learn to see setbacks not as failures but as opportunities to adapt and grow. Whether it's recovering from job loss, debt, or an unexpected expense, resilience comes from the ability to pivot, seek support, and stay focused on long-term goals. Celebrating small victories, like paying off a loan, completing a course, or securing a new client, builds confidence and reinforces the belief that progress is possible, even in challenging circumstances.

At its core, building financial independence is about reclaiming power in a system designed to strip it away. By saving strategically, earning creatively, and fostering collective support, women can challenge the economic structures that seek to exploit them. This is not just about surviving, it's about creating a foundation for autonomy, dignity, and freedom. The path is not easy, but with each step forward, women rewrite the rules of a system that was never meant to serve them. They prove, time and again, that even in the harshest conditions, independence is possible, and that their futures are theirs to define.

Organization and Productivity Apps

Trello

A project management tool that helps women organize tasks, track goals, and collaborate on projects. Trello's visual boards make it easy to prioritize and manage personal or professional tasks effectively.

Notion

A comprehensive organizational app combining note-taking, project tracking, and task management. It allows women to structure everything from daily routines to financial plans in one place.

Cozi

A family organizer app that helps manage shared calendars, shopping lists, and to-do lists. Perfect for women balancing work, family, and personal commitments.

Google Keep

A straightforward app for capturing notes, creating checklists, and setting reminders. Women can use it to keep track of ideas, manage tasks, or store inspiration on the go.

Financial Independence and Budgeting Apps

Mint
A budgeting app that tracks expenses, sets savings goals, and helps women manage their financial health by providing a complete overview of their finances.

YNAB (You Need A Budget)
A proactive budgeting tool designed to help users allocate their income toward financial goals. Women can use it to build savings, pay off debt, and gain financial stability.

Acorns
An investment app that rounds up purchases to the nearest dollar and invests the spare change. It's a beginner-friendly way for women to start building wealth through micro-investments.

Ellevest
A financial platform tailored for women, offering investment accounts, retirement planning, and financial coaching to help women achieve their financial goals.

Honeydue
A budgeting app designed for couples but also useful for women managing shared expenses or learning better financial communication skills.

Fiverr
A freelancing platform where women can monetize their skills, from graphic design to writing, allowing them to diversify income streams and gain financial independence.

These apps empower women to stay organized, manage their finances, and build a solid foundation for independence and growth.

Surviving/Thriving in the Post America Hellscape
13~Raising Rebels

Raising children to be critical thinkers and compassionate leaders in a world increasingly hostile to both is a delicate balance between resistance and protection. Project 2025's authoritarian policies don't just target adults; they aim to indoctrinate the next generation, ensuring conformity and obedience while erasing curiosity and dissent. For parents committed to challenging this oppressive system, the goal isn't just to raise children who survive but to raise rebels who question authority, champion justice, and build a better future. Part one of this chapter focuses on cultivating critical thinking and compassion while creating a home environment that nurtures curiosity, resilience, and safety.

The cornerstone of raising rebels is teaching children to think critically. Authoritarian systems rely on suppressing independent thought, and one of the most effective ways to resist is to question everything. This doesn't mean encouraging reckless defiance but fostering the ability to analyze and evaluate the world around them. Start by modeling this behavior at home. When discussing current events or even household rules, invite questions and engage in dialogue. If your child asks why a particular law exists or why a school policy seems unfair, use it as an opportunity to explore the reasoning behind it. Ask open-ended questions like, "Who benefits from this rule?" or "How might it affect different people?" Teaching children to think critically isn't about providing answers but encouraging exploration.

A critical component of this education is media literacy. Children are constantly exposed to information, much of it designed to manipulate or mislead. Help them learn to evaluate sources, recognize bias, and question narratives. This can be as simple as analyzing advertisements together, discussing how they appeal to emotions or create false needs. When watching the news, ask your child to consider what's being reported and what might be missing. "What are they not telling us?" is a powerful question that can help them recognize framing and omissions. Teaching media literacy equips children to navigate a world where propaganda often masquerades as truth.

Alongside critical thinking, compassion must be at the heart of raising rebels. Critical thinking without empathy risks creating cynicism, while compassion without critical thinking can leave children vulnerable to exploitation. Teach children to see the humanity in everyone, even those who act in harmful ways. Discuss the systemic roots of oppression and injustice, helping them understand that while individuals make choices, they often do so within deeply entrenched systems. This dual perspective encourages both accountability and empathy, allowing children to critique actions without dehumanizing others.

Compassion can also be cultivated through action. Encourage your children to participate in small acts of kindness, like helping a neighbor, volunteering at a local shelter, or standing up for a friend. These experiences help them see the impact of their choices and foster a sense of responsibility toward others. Storytelling is another powerful tool for building empathy. Share stories of people who have fought for justice, highlighting both their struggles and triumphs. Choose books and movies that celebrate underdog heroes and explore moral dilemmas, prompting discussions about courage, fairness, and community.

Creating a home environment that nurtures these qualities is essential. Authoritarian regimes thrive on fear and isolation, but a home filled with open dialogue, mutual respect, and curiosity offers a counterbalance. Establish family rituals that reinforce these values, whether it's discussing a thought-provoking question over dinner, hosting regular "family debates" on current issues, or reading books together that challenge conventional thinking. These rituals not only deepen bonds but also create a safe space where children feel empowered to express themselves without fear of judgment.

To protect children in a hostile society, parents must teach them to navigate the fine line between resistance and safety. This begins with helping them understand the difference between public and private spaces. In private, they can express their thoughts and frustrations freely. In public, however, they may need to practice discretion. Teach them how to express dissent in ways that minimize risk, such as through subtle symbols, coded language, or by aligning with trusted allies. Role-playing scenarios can help them prepare for challenging situations, like being asked to conform to a rule they disagree with. Practice responses that balance honesty with self-preservation, emphasizing that sometimes resistance requires patience and strategy.

Building intergenerational resilience is another vital aspect of raising rebels. Resistance is not new; it's a legacy passed down through generations, each building on the struggles and victories of those who came before. Share family stories of resilience, whether it's a great-grandparent who survived hardship or a relative who stood up for what was right. Connect these stories to larger historical movements, showing children that they are part of a broader tradition of resistance. This context not only inspires pride but also reinforces the idea that change is possible, even in the face of immense challenges.

Equally important is connecting children to a community of like-minded peers and mentors. Seek out clubs, groups, or organizations that align with your family's values, providing opportunities for collective learning and action. Whether it's a youth advocacy group, an environmental club, or a community theater project that tackles social issues, these spaces help children see the power of collaboration. They also normalize resistance, showing children that questioning authority and working for justice are not acts of rebellion but responsibilities of engaged citizens.

As children grow, their capacity for independence increases, and parents must adapt their approach. Adolescents, in particular, are keenly aware of injustice but often struggle to channel their emotions constructively. Support them by providing tools to take meaningful action, whether it's writing letters to local representatives, organizing a fundraiser for a cause they care about, or participating in peaceful protests. Help them see that resistance can take many forms, from public demonstrations to quiet acts of defiance, and that each has its place in the broader fight for justice.

Raising rebels is not just about preparing children to survive in a hostile world; it's about empowering them to challenge it. By cultivating critical thinking, compassion, and a sense of community, parents lay the foundation for the next generation of leaders and changemakers. In a world that demands compliance, every question asked, every act of kindness, and every stand taken becomes a beacon of hope. The fight for a better future begins at home, with parents who refuse to accept the status quo and children who dare to imagine something more.

As children grow, so too does their capacity to understand complexity and take meaningful action. The second part of raising rebels focuses on cultivating independence, deepening connections to history and community, and preparing children for the inevitable challenges of resistance. In the shadow of authoritarianism, raising critically-minded, empathetic, and resilient young people is both a strategy for survival and an investment in the future.

Teenagers, with their burgeoning sense of justice and identity, are particularly poised to become powerful agents of change. However, they often face a world that dismisses their perspectives or punishes their defiance. Parents must navigate this stage with care, providing both guidance and space for exploration. Engage adolescents in conversations about power dynamics, systems of oppression, and the ways these structures shape their own lives. Encourage them to articulate their observations and frustrations, helping them refine their critical thinking skills. This is also an ideal time to introduce them to the concept of intersectionality, showing how various forms of oppression, such as racism, sexism, and economic inequality, intersect and reinforce one another. Understanding these connections equips them to see the bigger picture and approach issues with greater empathy and insight.

Fostering independence is a delicate balance between granting freedom and providing a safety net. Encourage teenagers to take ownership of their resistance efforts, whether that means researching issues they care about, joining advocacy groups, or organizing small-scale initiatives like clothing drives or letter-writing campaigns. Support their endeavors by offering resources, brainstorming strategies, or simply being a sounding board for their ideas. At the same time, teach them to assess risks and develop contingency plans. For instance, if they're attending a protest, discuss what to do if the event takes a dangerous turn, including identifying safe exits and having a trusted contact on standby.

Community remains a vital source of strength for young rebels. Encourage them to seek out like-minded peers who share their values and aspirations. This might involve joining clubs, youth organizations, or online forums dedicated to activism and social justice. These connections not only reinforce their sense of purpose but also remind them that they are not alone in their struggles. For parents, fostering these relationships means providing opportunities and encouragement while remaining mindful of safety concerns, particularly in online spaces.

As part of their education, introduce teenagers to the stories of historical and contemporary resistance. These narratives serve as both inspiration and instruction, showing the strategies, sacrifices, and successes of those who have challenged injustice before them. Highlight diverse voices, ensuring they understand that resistance is not confined to a single demographic or ideology. Share biographies of figures like Harriet Tubman, Malala Yousafzai, or César Chávez, and connect their struggles to the current issues your family faces. Emphasize that while these individuals are celebrated, their victories were part of broader movements that relied on collective effort.

Art and storytelling are particularly powerful tools for engaging teenagers in resistance. Encourage them to express their frustrations and aspirations through creative outlets, whether it's writing, painting, filmmaking, or music. Art allows them to process complex emotions, challenge dominant narratives, and inspire others without necessarily putting themselves at risk. Support their creative endeavors by providing supplies, showcasing their work, or connecting them with mentors who can help them refine their skills. These acts of creation are not just cathartic, they are acts of rebellion in a world that often seeks to suppress imagination and dissent.

Financial literacy is another critical skill for young rebels. Economic independence provides a foundation for resistance, freeing them from dependence on systems that may exploit or control them. Teach them to budget, save, and make informed financial decisions, emphasizing the importance of building a safety net for the future. Encourage entrepreneurial thinking, such as starting small businesses or freelance projects that align with their passions and values. These ventures not only provide practical experience but also show them that self-reliance is possible, even in a predatory economy.

Navigating authority is a skill every young rebel must master. Teach teenagers how to interact with figures of power, whether teachers, employers, or law enforcement, in ways that assert their rights while minimizing conflict. Role-play scenarios to help them practice staying calm, articulate, and confident in high-pressure situations. Equip them with knowledge about their legal rights and responsibilities, ensuring they understand both the risks and rewards of resistance.

Resilience, both emotional and physical, is essential for enduring the challenges of standing up to authority. Help your children develop coping mechanisms to manage stress and setbacks, such as mindfulness practices, journaling, or physical activities like yoga or hiking. Encourage them to build strong support networks, including friends, family, and mentors who can provide encouragement and perspective during difficult times. Remind them that resistance is a long game, and setbacks are not failures but opportunities to regroup and strategize.

Finally, empower your children to dream of a better world. Authoritarian systems thrive on the suppression of imagination, convincing people that the status quo is inevitable. Counter this by fostering an environment where your children feel free to envision alternatives. Ask them to articulate their vision of justice, equality, or sustainability, and explore what steps might bring those visions closer to reality. These exercises not only inspire hope but also remind them of their agency and potential to shape the future.

Raising rebels in an authoritarian society is no small task, but it is one of the most powerful forms of resistance. By teaching critical thinking, fostering compassion, and building resilience, parents prepare the next generation to not only survive but to lead. These young people are not just inheriting a world in turmoil, they are shaping the path forward, carrying the legacy of resistance while forging their own. In a world that demands obedience, raising a child who dares to question, care, and act is a revolutionary act in itself. Together, across generations, families become the architects of a brighter, freer future.

Up next on the Christian nationalist agenda, shockingly but unsurprisingly, is the repeal of the 19th Amendment, the constitutional guarantee of women's right to vote. While this may seem like an unfathomable regression, it is a logical extension of the movement's broader aim to strip women of autonomy and return them to a subservient role in society. The effort to undo over a century of progress is not just a fringe fantasy but a calculated strategy to consolidate power by silencing a key demographic that has consistently challenged the patriarchal and authoritarian vision of Project 2025. For the leaders of this movement, women's voices at the ballot box represent a direct threat to their theocratic goals. By removing women from the democratic process, they aim to weaken the coalitions that have fought for justice and equity, ensuring that the policies of control and subjugation can proceed unopposed. If we do not want our daughters, let alone ourselves, losing our most important right, to have a voice in our democracy, we must acknowledge there really is no end game.

Say what you will about the Christian nationalist movement, they are relentless, like the Terminator, relentless in their pursuit of control, unyielding in their push for power, and tireless in their efforts to reshape society in their image. They do not stop; they do not compromise; they do not waver. What was unthinkable yesterday becomes today's extreme, and tomorrow's inevitable. A 15-week abortion ban, once viewed as a severe restriction, is quickly reframed as a reasonable middle ground, only for the conversation to shift again to a 6-week ban, and ultimately to a total prohibition. The Reek regime, under constant pressure to appease its Christian nationalist overlords, continues to shift the goalposts, feeding their insatiable appetite for cultural and political dominance. This normalization of extremism is their most insidious weapon.

By continually pushing the boundaries of what is acceptable, they condition society to accept what once seemed outrageous, exploiting compromise as a means to achieve their ultimate ends. They do not see their victories as final but as incremental steps toward an all-encompassing theocratic vision, where every policy tightens their grip on power and every "compromise" lays the groundwork for the next assault on freedom. It is this relentless march, this refusal to stop or slow down, that makes their agenda so dangerous, and so imperative to resist. All the more reason to ensure our kids are prepared to recognize this erosion of rights and equipped to fight for human rights for all.

Surviving/Thriving in the Post America Hellscape 14~Fighting Isolation with Community

Isolation is one of the most effective tools of authoritarian regimes. It fragments individuals, cutting them off from collective strength and solidarity. Under Project 2025, policies and cultural shifts are designed to create a society where people feel disconnected, helpless, and wary of one another. Isolation breeds fear and compliance, making it easier for those in power to control and exploit. In contrast, connection, building community, finding allies, and fostering mutual care, becomes an act of resistance. Community offers not only practical support but also the emotional strength to endure and push back against oppression. The first part of this chapter explores why isolation is their weapon, how connection can be your shield, and how to begin finding allies in the most unlikely places.

Isolation works because it preys on fundamental human vulnerabilities. The more disconnected people feel, the easier it is for fear and mistrust to take root. This disconnection is fostered by propaganda that sows division, policies that criminalize collective action, and a culture that valorizes individualism over solidarity. In this environment, people are conditioned to see one another as threats or competitors rather than allies. The regime benefits from this fragmentation, as it diverts attention away from systemic injustices and reduces the risk of organized resistance.

But even in such a climate, the power of community persists. Connection counters isolation by reminding people of their shared humanity and collective strength. Community offers a space where individuals can feel seen, heard, and valued, providing the emotional and practical resources needed to navigate challenging times. In a world designed to divide, finding and fostering these connections becomes a vital act of defiance.

The first step in fighting isolation is recognizing its presence and purpose. Authoritarian systems rely on more than just physical separation, they also cultivate psychological and emotional isolation. This can manifest as a reluctance to share vulnerabilities, a fear of speaking out, or a sense that no one else understands your struggles.

Acknowledging these feelings and understanding their origins is critical. They are not personal failings but deliberate tactics used to undermine solidarity.

Once you recognize isolation's grip, the next step is to reach out, even when it feels difficult or risky. Allies can often be found in unexpected places. Start by looking for shared experiences or values, even among people you may not know well. A coworker who shares your frustrations about workplace conditions, a neighbor who also misses the community library, or a fellow parent at your child's school who worries about changes in the curriculum, these are all potential allies. Small acts of openness, like a kind word or a question about someone's experiences, can lay the foundation for deeper connections.

Finding allies doesn't mean everyone will agree on every issue, and that's okay. Community doesn't require complete alignment of beliefs but a shared commitment to supporting one another and working toward common goals. Be willing to listen and learn from others, even when their perspectives differ from your own. Building trust and understanding takes time, but these connections are worth the effort.

In seeking allies, it's important to assess trust and boundaries carefully, particularly in a climate of surveillance and suspicion. Not everyone will be ready to form deeper connections, and some may inadvertently or intentionally pose risks to your safety. Look for people who demonstrate integrity, empathy, and a willingness to collaborate. Start with small, low-risk acts of cooperation, like sharing information, resources, or time, and gradually build a foundation of mutual trust.

Community can also be found in spaces where people naturally gather. Religious groups, schools, workplaces, and hobby clubs are all potential sources of connection, even if they seem apolitical at first glance. These settings often bring together individuals with diverse perspectives but shared needs, offering fertile ground for conversations that lead to collective action. For example, a church group might organize a food drive, which can evolve into a broader discussion about food insecurity in your area. A workplace lunch group might start as casual camaraderie but grow into a support network for addressing labor issues. By being present and engaged in these spaces, you can identify opportunities to build solidarity and work together toward shared goals.

Fostering community requires active effort and intention. It's not enough to hope connections will happen organically, you must take steps to create and nurture them. Start small, focusing on one-on-one relationships or small groups before scaling up. For example, invite a neighbor for coffee to discuss shared concerns or organize a book club to explore themes of resilience and justice. These initial connections can serve as the building blocks for larger networks.

As connections grow, so does the potential for mutual aid and collective action. Mutual aid networks are groups of people who come together to share resources, skills, and support based on principles of solidarity rather than charity. Unlike traditional charity models, which often reinforce power imbalances, mutual aid emphasizes reciprocity and empowerment. Everyone in the network is both a giver and a receiver, contributing what they can and receiving what they need.

The process of forming a mutual aid group begins with identifying shared needs and resources within your community. This might involve conducting informal surveys, hosting listening sessions, or simply paying attention to the challenges your neighbors face. Once you have a sense of these needs, gather a small group of trusted individuals to brainstorm ways to address them collectively. Start with manageable projects, such as coordinating transportation to medical appointments, organizing childcare swaps, or creating a shared pantry for food and supplies.

In addition to practical support, mutual aid networks provide a powerful antidote to isolation. They create spaces where people can share their experiences, celebrate victories, and process challenges together. This sense of belonging is crucial for sustaining resistance and resilience. When people feel connected and supported, they are better equipped to face the systemic forces arrayed against them.

Building community and mutual aid doesn't just fight isolation, it also lays the groundwork for broader resistance. Authoritarian regimes thrive on the idea that individuals are powerless against the system. By coming together, communities demonstrate that collective action is not only possible but also effective. Every small act of solidarity, whether it's sharing a meal, offering a ride, or standing up for a neighbor, strengthens the bonds that make larger movements possible.

In a world designed to isolate and divide, community becomes a revolutionary force. It reminds us that we are not alone, that our struggles are shared, and that our power lies in connection. By finding allies, fostering trust, and building mutual aid networks, we create not just a shield against isolation but a foundation for change. Together, we can face the challenges of authoritarianism and work toward a future where no one has to stand alone.

Mutual aid networks are more than lifelines, they are acts of defiance against the isolation and fragmentation authoritarian regimes depend on. These networks thrive on connection and reciprocity, providing immediate support while laying the foundation for long-term resilience. At their core is the belief that everyone has something to offer, whether it's time, skills, or resources, and that collective care is stronger than individual struggle. By organizing around shared needs, communities create spaces where people can reclaim agency and solidarity in the face of systemic oppression.

Scaling up mutual aid efforts requires structure without rigidity. Clear communication, regular check-ins, and defined roles allow these networks to remain adaptable while meeting the evolving needs of their members. Events like shared meals, resource swaps, or educational workshops deepen trust and foster collaboration. These gatherings are more than logistical, they create bonds of empathy and shared purpose, reminding participants that their struggles and successes are interconnected. Transparency and inclusivity in decision-making build trust, ensuring that everyone feels valued and empowered.

For mutual aid to be sustainable, communities must address both immediate crises and systemic issues. While providing food, childcare, or healthcare may be urgent priorities, longer-term solutions, like forming cooperatives or advocating for structural change, amplify the network's impact. These efforts challenge the narrative that survival is a solitary endeavor, proving instead that solidarity and care are transformative forces. Mutual aid networks don't just counteract isolation; they rewrite the story of resistance, demonstrating that even in the darkest times, connection can foster hope, resilience, and a path toward a more equitable future. Together, communities become both shields against oppression and the architects of a brighter, freer world.

Social community apps- Independently owned, not tied to major platforms like Zuckerberg's Meta or Musk's ventures

Mastodon
A decentralized social networking platform where users join servers tailored to specific interests or communities.
Offers a user-controlled experience, free from corporate oversight. It's particularly valued for fostering niche communities and meaningful interactions.

Hive Social
A user-friendly, independently developed social app blending features of Twitter and Instagram.
Focuses on creating a non-toxic environment with chronological feeds and creative expression without heavy algorithms.

Vero
A subscription-based social network emphasizing privacy and ad-free interaction.
Prioritizes authentic connections and visual content without exploiting user data or injecting ads.

WT.Social
A non-profit, ad-free social network created by Wikipedia co-founder Jimmy Wales.
Focuses on fostering community-driven discussions with an emphasis on accurate, meaningful content.

Amino
A community-based platform where users can join and create interest-based groups.
Encourages niche community building, making it easy to connect with like-minded people through discussions, polls, and collaborative projects.

These apps, and the open protocol *Nostr,* provide refreshing alternatives to large, corporate-owned platforms, offering diverse ways to engage with communities in a more personal and secure manner.

Surviving/Thriving in the Post America Hellscape 15~Laughing in the Face of Tyranny

In the darkest of times, when oppression and authoritarianism tighten their grip, laughter becomes more than a momentary reprieve, it becomes a weapon. Gallows humor, satire, and mockery have long been used to undermine power, challenge authority, and offer a spark of hope in seemingly hopeless situations. Authoritarian regimes thrive on control and fear, but laughter is something they can never fully suppress. It exposes the absurdity of their rhetoric, punctures their self-importance, and reminds the oppressed that even in their harshest moments, they retain something untouchable: their ability to see through the facade and find strength in humor. Part one of this chapter explores gallows humor as a survival mechanism and delves into the power of satire to strip tyranny of its veneer of invincibility.

Humor, particularly the dark and biting kind, has always been a natural response to oppression. It allows people to articulate fears and frustrations that might otherwise be dangerous to voice directly. Jokes, memes, and satirical stories can say what protests or essays cannot, offering a subversive outlet for dissent. Gallows humor doesn't ignore the pain or horror of the moment, it acknowledges it, meets it head-on, and dares to laugh at its absurdity. This act of laughing in the face of tyranny becomes a form of defiance, a reminder that no matter how oppressive a regime may be, it can never fully own the minds or spirits of the people. Humor makes suffering bearable, builds camaraderie among the oppressed, and signals to the oppressors that they are not as powerful as they would like to believe.

The use of satire takes this defiance to another level, turning humor into a scalpel that cuts through propaganda and exposes the contradictions and hypocrisies of authoritarian regimes. Satire has always been a thorn in the side of those in power. From the biting wit of Jonathan Swift's *A Modest Proposal* to the irreverent caricatures of 20th-century political cartoonists, satire thrives on showing the ridiculousness of the ruling class. In authoritarian regimes, where control over public narratives is paramount, satire becomes even more powerful. It disrupts the regime's attempt to present itself as infallible, offering a counter-narrative that mocks their authority and reveals their flaws. For oppressed people, satire is not just funny, it's empowering. It says, "We see through your lies, and we are not afraid to call them out."

Historically, humor has been a lifeline for resistance movements. During World War II, underground groups across Europe used humor to mock Nazi propaganda and ridicule collaborators. Resistance newspapers, graffiti, and even whispered jokes became ways to undermine the image of Nazi invincibility. One joke, popular in occupied countries, quipped, "What will we do after the war? Declare the Germans insane and give them freedom of movement!" Such humor didn't change policies overnight, but it chipped away at the psychological power of occupation, reminding people that the oppressors were not gods, they were human, flawed, and beatable. In the Soviet Union, samizdat (underground publications) frequently included satirical poems, cartoons, and absurdist stories that poked fun at the rigid bureaucracy and propaganda of the regime. These works, though often circulated at great personal risk, provided an outlet for frustration and a shared sense of rebellion.

The power of humor lies not only in its ability to critique but also in its capacity to unify. A shared laugh creates bonds of solidarity among those who feel isolated by oppression. Humor becomes a code, a way for people to signal their resistance without overtly declaring it. A sharp-witted remark in a factory line, a satirical poster pasted on a wall, or a whispered joke in a schoolyard can bring people together, creating pockets of resistance in environments otherwise steeped in fear. This shared experience of laughter reinforces the idea that the regime's control is not total, that dissent still lives in the hearts and minds of the people.

In contemporary times, humor continues to be a potent force against authoritarianism. In oppressive societies, satire and comedy often migrate online, where they spread rapidly and reach audiences that traditional forms of resistance cannot. Memes, videos, and satirical articles thrive on social media, bypassing censors and challenging propaganda with wit and irreverence. In places like Belarus, Iran, and Hong Kong, humor has become a crucial tool for activists to critique authoritarian figures, mock state narratives, and rally support for their movements. A single meme can capture the absurdity of a regime's policies or the hubris of its leaders in a way that resonates across cultural and linguistic barriers.

However, humor in oppressive regimes is not without risk. Authoritarian leaders understand its power and often crack down harshly on those who wield it. Cartoonists, satirists, and comedians have faced imprisonment, exile, or even death for daring to ridicule those in power. Yet, this suppression only underscores how deeply humor threatens the foundations of tyranny. A regime that cannot tolerate jokes is a regime that knows its grip is tenuous, its image fragile, and its authority dependent on fear rather than respect. Each act of humor, then, becomes a small act of rebellion, a reminder that even in the most repressive environments, the human spirit remains unbroken.

For those living under Project 2025, gallows humor and satire are essential tools for survival and resistance. The Reek regime, with its bombastic rhetoric, draconian policies, and cartoonishly self-important leaders, is ripe for ridicule. Memes mocking their authoritarian overreach, satirical stories exposing the contradictions in their policies, and darkly funny observations about the absurdities of daily life under their rule all serve to puncture the facade of invincibility they seek to project. For those oppressed by their policies, laughter is not just a release, it is a declaration of defiance. It says, "You may control many things, but you will never control our ability to see through you, to mock you, and to find joy in the face of your attempts to crush us."

Gallows humor is not a substitute for other forms of resistance, but it is a vital complement to them. It sustains spirits, builds solidarity, and reminds people that they still have power, even if it's the power to laugh. It is a small but profound act of rebellion, one that turns the weight of oppression into a moment of levity and light. In a world where everything feels heavy, humor offers a lifeline, a reminder that no matter how dark things may seem, there is still a spark of humanity that refuses to be extinguished.

Laughter has always been a profound form of rebellion, particularly in the most oppressive regimes. Humor doesn't just provide temporary relief; it disrupts the narratives of those in power, exposing their absurdity and undermining their authority. In the face of Project

2025's authoritarian policies, satire and gallows humor serve as tools for both survival and organized resistance. Part two of this chapter examines contemporary humor-as-resistance movements, strategies for using humor effectively, and the ways in which satire fosters solidarity while keeping the flame of dissent alive.

One of the most striking examples of humor in contemporary resistance comes from Belarus during the 2020 anti-government protests. Protesters used humor not only to critique President Alexander Lukashenko's authoritarian rule but also to make their demonstrations accessible and engaging to a wider audience. A group of women, dubbed "The Ladies in White," dressed in white and carried flowers, blending satire with peaceful protest. Another widely shared image featured a group of protesters holding a sign that read, "Go away, please, and thank you," using politeness as a biting critique of Lukashenko's brutality. These humorous gestures added an element of levity to the protests, capturing global attention and making the movement feel less intimidating for those hesitant to join.

Similarly, during the Arab Spring, humor played a critical role in mobilizing young people and breaking down fear. In Egypt, jokes and memes about then-President Hosni Mubarak proliferated across social media, turning the leader's attempts at controlling the narrative into fodder for widespread ridicule. The phrase "Leave, my hand hurts from holding this sign" became a common joke among protesters, highlighting the absurdity of Mubarak's refusal to step down. The humor didn't just entertain, it encouraged people to see the regime as less omnipotent and made participation in the resistance feel like a communal act of catharsis.

In Hong Kong, during the 2019 protests against the Chinese government, humor became a critical weapon against fear and surveillance. Protesters donned absurd costumes, including inflatable Pikachu suits and Guy Fawkes masks, while creating satirical art that mocked the Chinese government. One widely circulated image depicted a cartoon Xi Jinping as Winnie the Pooh, a reference to the Chinese leader's sensitivity about the comparison. These humorous acts carried real risk, yet they became rallying points for solidarity. Humor diffused fear turned the oppressors into the butt of the joke, and allowed protesters to assert control over the narrative.

Closer to home, satire has been a mainstay in critiquing authoritarian tendencies within the United States. Late-night comedians, satirical news programs, and online platforms like *The Onion* have long used humor to call out hypocrisy and hold the powerful accountable. However, as authoritarianism deepens, these forms of humor take on new significance. Memes mocking the contradictions of Project 2025 policies, satirical videos exposing the absurdity of the Reek regime's propaganda, and comedic commentary on their overreach have the power to reach audiences that traditional journalism might not. Humor becomes a language of dissent, accessible and engaging even for those who might not otherwise feel politically inclined.

For individuals living under such regimes, using humor effectively requires creativity and subtlety. Direct attacks on authoritarian figures often come with significant risk, so dissenters frequently rely on indirect or coded humor. This might involve creating jokes that are open to interpretation, allowing plausible deniability if questioned. For example, a joke about "a king with no clothes" could easily be passed off as a general observation while resonating with those who understand its true meaning. Similarly, humor that focuses on the absurdity of daily life under the regime, rather than directly targeting its leaders, can be a safer yet equally powerful way to resist.

Community humor, shared within trusted circles, is another strategy for using satire while minimizing risk. In this context, humor becomes a way to bond and build resilience among those who are oppressed. Private joke-sharing sessions, humorous skits at underground meetings, or even graffiti in hidden locations can foster a sense of solidarity. The knowledge that others are laughing with you, even in dire circumstances, creates a sense of belonging and shared purpose.

It's also important to recognize the role of art and storytelling in humor-as-resistance. Cartoons, memes, and satirical plays allow for a more visual and emotional connection to the critique. A single image, cleverly designed, can encapsulate the hypocrisy of a policy or the arrogance of a leader more effectively than a detailed argument. Satirical art is particularly powerful because it transcends language barriers and can be shared widely, both online and offline. Artists, writers, and performers have a unique role in resistance movements, using their creativity to make oppression not just visible but laughable.

In building humor-based resistance, the role of digital platforms cannot be overstated. Social media allows humor to spread quickly and reach audiences far beyond the immediate community. Hashtags, viral memes, and humorous videos amplify the voices of those resisting, often garnering international attention. However, the digital realm also carries risks, particularly in regimes with advanced surveillance capabilities. Activists must balance the desire for visibility with the need for security, using anonymized accounts, encrypted platforms, and other tools to protect themselves.

While humor is a powerful tool, it must be wielded thoughtfully. Poorly executed humor can alienate potential allies or inadvertently reinforce harmful stereotypes. Effective humor-as-resistance must punch up, targeting those in power rather than marginalized groups. It should unite rather than divide, reminding people of their shared humanity and collective strength. At its best, humor is both incisive and inclusive, creating a space where even those who disagree can engage with its message.

Perhaps most importantly, humor offers hope. In environments where despair and fear threaten to overwhelm, the ability to laugh is a reminder of resilience. Laughter doesn't erase the pain or injustice of oppression, but it provides a moment of relief, a way to reclaim joy and agency even in the darkest circumstances. It reminds people that they are more than victims, they are thinkers, creators, and rebels who can see through the facade of power and refuse to take it too seriously.

Gallows humor and satire have always been the quiet undercurrent of resistance movements, offering a means to survive, critique, and connect. Whether it's a whispered joke, a viral meme, or a satirical performance, humor chips away at the foundations of tyranny, one laugh at a time. For those living under Project 2025, humor may seem like a small act, but its impact is profound. It keeps the spirit of dissent alive, fosters solidarity, and reminds the oppressors that their power is far from absolute. In a world where so much feels beyond control, the ability to laugh in the face of tyranny is a victory in itself, a spark of freedom that no regime can extinguish.

Traditional Creativity & Artistic Inspiration

The Artist's Way by Julia Cameron
Journaling, daily practices, and connecting with inner artistry.
Steal Like an Artist by Austin Kleon
Approachable advice on creativity, blending analog and digital worlds.
Big Magic: Creative Living Beyond Fear by Elizabeth Gilbert
Overcoming self-doubt to embrace creative freedom.
Creative Confidence by Tom Kelley & David Kelley
Design thinking and innovation as everyday tools.
Drawing on the Right Side of the Brain by Betty Edwards
Traditional art techniques as gateways to creativity.

Modern Creativity & Digital Tools

Show Your Work! by Austin Kleon
Creative entrepreneurship in the digital age.
Creative Calling by Chase Jarvis
Building creative habits and leveraging technology to amplify ideas.
The Art of Digital Design by Patrick McNeil
Merging traditional design principles with digital media.
Make Time: How to Focus on What Matters Every Day by Jake Knapp & John Zeratsky
Balancing modern digital life with creative focus.
The War of Art by Steven Pressfield
Breaking through creative barriers in any medium.

For Both Traditional and Digital Creators

Keep Going by Austin Kleon
Staying creative and motivated, regardless of obstacles.
Digital Minimalism by Cal Newport
Leveraging technology without letting it consume you.
Understanding Comics: The Invisible Art by Scott McCloud
Storytelling techniques applicable to both physical and digital media.
The Creative Habit by Twyla Tharp
Translating creative discipline to any medium, from dance to digital.
Learning by Heart: Teachings to Free the Creative Spirit by Corita Kent & Jan Steward
Encouraging play and exploration in creative work.

Surviving/Thriving in the Post America Hellscape
16~Civil Disobedience & Everyday Resistance

In the shadow of authoritarianism, resistance often requires quiet, deliberate acts that challenge oppression without drawing dangerous attention. Civil disobedience and everyday resistance take on a new dimension in a surveillance state, where every move may be watched, recorded, or used against you. The methods may vary, but the purpose remains constant: to disrupt the systems of control, protect vulnerable communities, and maintain the spark of dissent in even the most repressive environments. Part one of this chapter focuses on what nonviolent resistance looks like in such a society, the power of small acts of defiance, and the balance between open confrontation and blending in.

Nonviolent resistance in a surveillance state begins with understanding the tools of the oppressor. Technology is often weaponized to monitor, manipulate, and intimidate, creating an environment where dissent feels perilous. Recognizing this reality, resistance becomes less about grand gestures and more about strategic, often invisible, defiance. This can include everything from refusing to comply with unjust rules to spreading truthful information in subtle, creative ways. It's about bending the oppressive system until it breaks, using methods that minimize risk while maximizing impact.

One of the most powerful forms of everyday resistance is the simple act of refusing to accept the narrative imposed by those in power. Authoritarian regimes rely on propaganda to create a facade of legitimacy, but citizens can undermine this narrative by sharing alternative stories and perspectives. In a surveillance state, this might mean passing handwritten notes instead of texting, sharing USB drives with banned articles, or using encryption to protect sensitive communications. These actions may seem small, but collectively they create cracks in the regime's control over information, allowing truth to seep through.

Economic noncooperation is another subtle yet effective tool. Boycotting regime-affiliated businesses, redirecting spending to support local or underground economies, and refusing to participate in exploitative systems all chip away at the foundations of authoritarian control. For example, workers might slow down productivity in ways that are difficult to trace, while consumers might quietly organize to starve state-run industries of revenue. These actions don't require large-scale coordination to be effective; even isolated acts, when multiplied across a population, can have a significant impact.

Public acts of defiance, though riskier, remain essential in keeping the spirit of resistance alive. In a surveillance state, these acts often take creative forms to evade detection or punishment. Street art, for instance, can be used to deliver powerful messages without revealing the identity of the artist. Anonymous posters, graffiti, or chalk messages that appear and disappear quickly can inspire hope and signal resistance without leaving a trail. Similarly, flash mobs or silent demonstrations that disperse before authorities can react can make a statement without exposing participants to significant danger.

While public defiance is critical, blending in can be equally powerful depending on the context. Resistance doesn't always require visible confrontation. Quietly subverting rules, sabotaging oppressive systems, or simply refusing to participate in harmful practices can be just as impactful. For instance, a teacher might continue teaching critical thinking skills despite a restrictive curriculum, or a government employee might discreetly protect sensitive information from misuse. These acts of defiance often go unnoticed by the regime but have profound ripple effects within the community.

Timing is crucial in deciding when to fight openly and when to blend in. Open resistance is most effective when there is collective momentum and a clear strategy for minimizing harm. In contrast, blending in is often necessary when the risks of exposure outweigh the potential gains of confrontation. Understanding this balance requires careful planning and situational awareness. Resistance is not about recklessness; it's about choosing battles wisely, protecting yourself and others while chipping away at the systems of oppression.

Even in a heavily surveilled society, communities can create safe spaces for resistance. These might be physical locations, like private homes or hidden meeting spots, or virtual spaces protected by encryption and anonymity. Within these spaces, people can organize, share resources, and build networks of trust. These connections are vital for sustaining resistance, providing the emotional and logistical support needed to continue the fight.

Nonviolent resistance in a surveillance state thrives on creativity and adaptability. Oppressors rely on predictability to maintain control, but resistance flourishes when it becomes unexpected, dynamic, and difficult to trace. Whether through anonymous acts of defiance, strategic economic noncooperation, or the quiet undermining of unjust systems, everyday resistance proves that even in the face of overwhelming power, people can find ways to push back. The small, subtle acts of defiance, multiplied across a population, become the foundation of larger movements, reminding everyone that resistance is possible, and that even in silence, dissent can be deafening.

Everyday resistance is not just about survival, it's about reclaiming humanity in the face of dehumanization. Authoritarian regimes thrive on fear, isolation, and the erosion of individual purpose and collective identity. To combat this, acts of resistance must not only disrupt systems of oppression but also nourish the spirit and strengthen community bonds. Art as activism and spiritual renewal are two powerful tools in this fight, offering ways to resist that are as sustaining as they are transformative.

Art has always been a weapon of resistance, capable of conveying messages that words alone cannot. Under authoritarian rule, where dissenting voices are silenced, art becomes an essential means of expression. A mural painted under the cover of night, a song shared quietly among friends, or even a handmade patch sewn onto a jacket can speak volumes. These creative acts challenge oppressive narratives while inspiring others to imagine alternatives. Art invites people to see beyond the bleakness of the present and envision a future free from tyranny, rekindling hope in the darkest moments.

In a surveillance state, where visibility can bring danger, anonymity often becomes part of the art itself. Street artists leave stencils or paste posters that critique the regime without revealing their identities. Poets and writers circulate their work through underground networks or encrypted platforms, and digital art spreads across borders as memes and graphics. These creations may not topple regimes on their own, but they undermine authoritarian control of cultural narratives, exposing cracks in their authority and fostering solidarity among those who recognize the message.

Art also serves as collective healing. Community projects such as quilt-making, collaborative murals, or group storytelling sessions allow individuals to process trauma and find strength in shared experiences. These acts of creation transform pain into something tangible and meaningful, reminding people that while authoritarian regimes may control institutions and resources, they cannot control the human drive to create, connect, and resist.

Spiritual renewal complements art by strengthening individuals from within. Oppressive systems drain people of their energy and hope, leaving them demoralized and compliant. Spiritual practices, whether rooted in religion, mindfulness, or personal rituals, offer a way to reclaim inner peace and resilience. Prayer, meditation, or quiet reflection provides space to process fear, grief, and frustration without being consumed by them. These moments of renewal are acts of defiance, reclaiming time and energy that the regime seeks to consume.

For some, spirituality might mean finding solace in nature, where the oppressive reach of authoritarianism feels less immediate. A walk through the woods, tending a garden, or sitting by a river can ground people in their connection to the natural world and offer perspective beyond the immediate struggles. For others, spiritual renewal might involve gathering with like-minded individuals to share intentions, affirm beliefs, or participate in rituals that strengthen collective bonds. These gatherings provide emotional fortitude, reminding participants of their shared values and purpose.

Spiritual practices also allow individuals to reframe their struggles. Resistance, often exhausting and fraught with setbacks, can feel overwhelming without a sense of purpose. Practices like journaling, prayer, or rituals help people reconnect with their values and the larger narrative of justice and liberation. This perspective transforms resistance from a series of isolated battles into a meaningful journey, infusing even the smallest acts of defiance with significance.

Together, art and spirituality create a powerful foundation for resistance. Art builds solidarity and amplifies voices, while spirituality provides the inner strength to persevere. These tools address both the external and internal challenges of living under authoritarian rule, reminding people of their shared humanity and their potential to shape a better future. Each mural, poem, and moment of reflection is a testament to the enduring power of the human spirit. These acts of resistance ripple outward, inspiring others and building the momentum necessary for meaningful change. Even in the harshest conditions, art and spirituality ensure that the seeds of freedom continue to grow.

Books for Peaceful Rebellion

Rules for Radicals by Saul Alinsky

Why Read It: A foundational text on grassroots organizing, this book offers strategic and creative approaches for challenging entrenched systems of power.
Key Themes: Community action, the dynamics of power, and tactical innovation.
Famous Insight: "Power is not only what you have but what the enemy thinks you have."

The Power of the Powerless by Václav Havel

Why Read It: A profound exploration of resistance under totalitarian regimes, focusing on how individuals can resist through truth and moral courage.
Key Themes: Dissent, integrity, and the subversive power of "living within the truth."
Famous Insight: "The system depends on people's willingness to live within a lie."

Why Civil Resistance Works: The Strategic Logic of Nonviolent Conflict by Erica Chenoweth and Maria J. Stephan

Why Read It: This research-backed book proves that nonviolent resistance is often more successful and sustainable than violent uprisings.
Key Themes: The power of nonviolence, mobilizing mass participation, and effective strategy.
Famous Insight: Nonviolent resistance attracts broader participation and is more likely to lead to durable success.

Surviving/Thriving in the Post America Hellscape
17~Preparing for the Worst

In an unstable world where disasters, whether natural, political, or economic, can strike at any moment, preparation is no longer a luxury but a necessity. Planning for the worst doesn't mean succumbing to paranoia or embracing the doomsday-prepper stereotype. Instead, it's about equipping yourself and your family with the tools, skills, and mindset needed to survive and adapt. Preparedness is an act of empowerment, ensuring that when the unexpected happens, you can face it with resilience and clarity. In part one, we'll explore what to pack, stash, and learn to ensure your family's survival.

The foundation of disaster preparedness is a well-thought-out go-bag, also known as a bug-out bag. This portable kit should contain the essentials needed to survive for at least 72 hours. Every member of your household, including children, should have their own tailored go-bag, but the contents should be lightweight enough to carry comfortably. Start with the basics: water and food. Pack a minimum of three liters of water per person and include water purification tablets or a portable filtration system. For food, focus on non-perishable, high-energy items like protein bars, nuts, and dehydrated meals. Compact and lightweight, these foods provide the necessary calories without taking up too much space.

Next, prioritize shelter and warmth. Include a compact sleeping bag or an emergency blanket, which can protect against hypothermia in harsh conditions. A lightweight tent or tarp, along with paracord, can be used to create temporary shelter. For clothing, pack layers that can be adjusted for different weather conditions, including moisture-wicking shirts, a waterproof jacket, and durable footwear. Gloves and a hat are also essential, as they help retain body heat in cold environments.

In terms of tools, your go-bag should include a multipurpose knife, a flashlight with extra batteries or a hand-crank model, and a lighter or waterproof matches. These tools can be used for a variety of survival tasks, from starting a fire to repairing gear. A basic first-aid kit is another non-negotiable. Include bandages, antiseptic wipes, pain relievers, and any prescription medications your family members require. Familiarize yourself with how to use each item; a well-stocked kit is useless if you don't know how to administer first aid.

Communication is another critical aspect of preparedness. In disaster scenarios, cell service and internet access are often the first things to go. Pack a portable radio to receive emergency broadcasts and consider investing in walkie-talkies or a satellite communication device to stay connected with your family or group. Keep a written list of important contacts, including family members, local emergency services, and trusted allies. In today's digital age, it's easy to rely on saved numbers, but having a physical backup ensures you're not stranded if your phone becomes inaccessible.

Beyond the go-bag, building a home survival kit is equally important. This kit should be designed for sheltering in place during disasters that don't require immediate evacuation, such as severe weather events or civil unrest. Stockpile at least two weeks' worth of food and water per person, focusing on shelf-stable items like canned goods, rice, and pasta. A manual can opener is essential for accessing canned foods. Don't forget pet supplies if you have animals; their needs are just as critical as your own.

Your home kit should also include hygiene supplies. In disasters, sanitation often becomes a major issue, leading to the spread of disease. Stock items like soap, hand sanitizer, feminine hygiene products, and portable toilets or buckets with liners. Personal protective equipment (PPE), such as gloves and masks, can also be invaluable in maintaining hygiene and safety, particularly during pandemics or chemical exposure scenarios.

Learning survival skills is another cornerstone of preparedness. Knowledge is the most portable and reliable tool you can carry. Start with basic skills like fire-starting, water purification, and food preservation. Take courses in first aid and CPR, or study reliable guides on wilderness survival. Even urban dwellers benefit from learning how to navigate without GPS, recognize edible plants, or create makeshift tools. Survival isn't just about the resources you have, it's about how you use them.

Flexibility and adaptability are critical mindsets in disaster planning. No plan will account for every variable, so the ability to improvise and adjust is essential. Regularly review and update your plans and supplies to ensure they remain relevant. Conduct family drills for different scenarios, evacuations, fire safety, or lockdowns, to ensure everyone knows what to do and where to go. These exercises not only improve readiness but also reduce panic when disaster strikes.

Finally, consider your mental and emotional preparedness. Disasters are not only physically demanding but also psychologically taxing. Build resilience by fostering strong relationships within your household and community. Talk openly about potential scenarios and discuss how you will support one another through them. Include items in your go-bag or home kit that provide comfort, such as a favorite book, a small toy for children, or a notebook for journaling. These small touches can make a significant difference in maintaining morale during stressful times.

Preparedness is not about living in fear but about taking proactive steps to ensure safety and stability in an unpredictable world. By assembling essential supplies, learning critical skills, and fostering a mindset of adaptability, you create a foundation of resilience for yourself and your family. The act of preparing is itself a form of resistance, a refusal to be caught off guard and a declaration that you will face whatever comes with courage and determination. In the next section, we will delve into strategies for staying mobile, protecting resources, and adapting to the changing landscapes of disaster scenarios.

Surviving/Thriving in the Post America Hellscape 18~Imagining a Post-Post America

In the bleakest of times, when authoritarianism casts its longest shadow, the act of imagining a better future is revolutionary. Project 2025 represents the culmination of a system designed to subjugate, silence, and control. Its architects fear women's power, despise our autonomy, and work tirelessly to erase us from the story. But their fear is justified. They know what we are capable of, and they should be afraid, because their time is finite, and ours is inevitable. The future does not belong to them, it belongs to us. Women's resilience will not only outlast their authoritarian nightmare but will build a world where their cruelty can never return. This chapter is about the long game, about the refusal to merely survive and the determination to thrive, take back power, and claim the whole pie this time.

Authoritarian regimes have always sought to crush women first. They see us as both the easiest targets and the greatest threats. They attack our rights, our bodies, our choices, believing that by controlling women, they can control the future. They pass laws that criminalize miscarriages, restrict our ability to work and live independently, and force us into roles designed to prop up their fragile egos. Their hatred is visceral because it is rooted in fear: fear of our ability to create, to organize, and to persist. But history has shown that no regime, no matter how oppressive, can keep women down forever. We adapt, we resist, and when the time comes, we rebuild.

The road to a post-Post America will not be easy, and it will not be short. They will come for us, again and again, with policies meant to strip us of autonomy and rhetoric meant to erode our confidence. But we are not fragile, and we are not alone. Every small victory, whether it's helping a neighbor access care, forming mutual aid networks, or exposing their lies, chips away at their power. These acts may seem insignificant in the moment, but they are the threads that weave the fabric of resistance. Together, these threads become unbreakable.

Rebuilding a better world requires reimagining everything they have tried to destroy. This time, there is no sharing power, no compromising with those who would see us subjugated. Women will not settle for a slice of the pie when we baked the whole thing. Our voices, our experiences, and our leadership must define the future, not as tokens, but as architects of a new system. The structures of power that enabled Project 2025 must be dismantled entirely. Patriarchy, capitalism unchecked by ethics, and systemic racism, all these interconnected forces must be unraveled and replaced with systems built on equity, compassion, and justice.

Hope in this struggle is not a passive thing; it is active, deliberate, and fierce. It comes from collective action, from seeing the faces of those who stand beside us, and from knowing that even in our darkest moments, we are building something better. It is the hope found in small victories, in the moments when we refuse to comply, when we speak truth despite the risks, and when we see our resistance inspire others. Hope is not naïve, it is a weapon. It is what keeps us moving forward, even when the path is obscured by fear and uncertainty.

Women's resilience is not a soft thing, it is hard-edged, unyielding, and born of necessity. We have carried the weight of oppression for centuries, and we know how to survive. But survival is not enough. This time, we fight for a world where our daughters do not have to bear the same burdens, where the systems that crush us are dismantled so thoroughly that they cannot rise again. This is the long game: not just enduring but winning, not just winning but transforming. We are not looking to restore what was, we are building what should have been all along.

In this future, there is no room for their hatred, no tolerance for their oppression. The systems that enabled their rise, unchecked corporate greed, the exploitation of the vulnerable, the silencing of dissent, will be dismantled. In their place, we will build systems that prioritize care over profit, equity over dominance, and humanity over power. This is not a utopian dream but a necessary reclamation. It is a future where women's voices are not marginalized but central, where our strength is not feared but celebrated, and where our leadership shapes a world that serves all, not just the privileged few.

The end of Project 2025's reign of terror will not be the end of the fight, it will be the beginning of a new chapter. Rebuilding will be hard, messy, and imperfect, but it will be ours. And we will not share it with those who hate us, those who have fought to erase us. This time, the future belongs entirely to us, because we are the ones who will make it. Women have always been the backbone of change, the ones who pick up the pieces and build anew. This time, we are not just picking up pieces; we are forging a new foundation, one that cannot be broken.

We are not waiting for permission to dream of this future. We are building it now, in every act of resistance, every bond of solidarity, and every moment of defiance. They hate us because they know we will win. And they are right to be afraid. The pie was always ours. This time, we take it all.

This is our time, and we will not squander it. The rebuilding of a post-Post America will be a labor of generations, but it starts now, with every small act of defiance, every refusal to yield, and every seed of hope planted in the ashes of their cruelty. Women's resilience is not just about survival; it's about creation. We have always been the creators, whether it's nurturing life, building communities, or imagining futures they couldn't fathom. This time, we create a world where our strength is no longer suppressed but celebrated.

To rebuild, we must begin with truth-telling. The regime's power was built on lies, lies about who we are, about what we deserve, and about what is possible. We will not let their propaganda shape the narrative of the future. Instead, we will tell our own stories, of resistance, survival, and triumph. These stories will not just honor the past but guide the path forward. They will teach us and future generations to recognize the tactics of oppression and to fight them with courage and clarity. Our stories are our power, and we will wield them unapologetically.

Justice will be another cornerstone of the world we create. The systems of oppression that allowed Project 2025 to flourish must be dismantled completely. This is not a time for reconciliation without accountability. Those who orchestrated and benefited from our suffering must face consequences, not out of vengeance, but to ensure that the lessons of this era are learned and embedded in the foundations of the future. True justice is not punitive alone; it is restorative. It seeks to heal the wounds inflicted by oppression and create systems that prevent those wounds from being reopened.

As we dismantle the old, we must also build the new. This means creating institutions that serve people, not power. Healthcare systems that prioritize human well-being over profit. Governments that reflect the diversity of their people, with women, people of color, and marginalized communities at the forefront. Economic systems that reward care work and community-building rather than exploitation and greed. These are not dreams, they are necessities. And they are within our reach if we approach this work with the same tenacity and ingenuity that have sustained us through their darkest days.

Community will be our foundation. The bonds formed in resistance will evolve into the networks that sustain rebuilding. We will build neighborhoods that care for their most vulnerable, schools that teach truth and empathy, and workplaces that value humanity over productivity. Mutual aid networks, born out of necessity, will remain as enduring symbols of what we can achieve together. This is not about returning to what was lost, it's about forging something entirely new.

And as we create, we will celebrate. Women know how to find joy even in the midst of struggle, and that joy will fuel our future. Every victory, no matter how small, will be a reminder of what we have overcome and what we are capable of. We will sing, dance, paint, and write the story of our triumph into the fabric of the world we rebuild. Joy is resistance, and it is also the foundation of resilience.

They will call us selfish for claiming what we've always deserved. They will say we are angry, that we are radical, that we demand too much. Let them. For generations, we have compromised, shrunk ourselves, and accepted less than what we are owed. No more. This time, we are not asking. We are taking back what is ours, unapologetically and without restraint. Their hatred, their fear, their cruelty, they all stem from their recognition of a truth they can no longer deny that when women lead, the world transforms. And this time, it transforms permanently, for the good of all but their oppressive designs.

The long game of rebuilding a post-Post America will not be easy, but it will be transformative. Every oppressive structure we dismantle, every institution we remake, every future we reimagine will bring us closer to the world we deserve, a world where justice and equity are not aspirations but foundations. This isn't just about reclaiming power; it's about ensuring that no one ever has to fight this battle again. It is about crafting a legacy of courage, compassion, and enduring hope for the generations that will follow. Women have always risen, but this time, we rise to lead, to rebuild, and to never fall again. This is our time, our revolution, and our chance to leave a mark so indelible that the echoes of our triumph will carry forward for centuries. We will not waste it. We will make it count.

Selection of books that imagine a peaceful future

The More Beautiful World Our Hearts Know Is Possible by Charles Eisenstein

Why Read It: This book explores the transition from a world defined by separation, competition, and scarcity to one built on interconnectedness, collaboration, and abundance.
Vision: A call for collective transformation and a deep belief in humanity's potential for creating a compassionate, peaceful tomorrow.

Ecotopia by Ernest Callenbach

Why Read It: A speculative novel set in a sustainable, eco-conscious utopia, it envisions a society that values environmental harmony, equality, and community.
Vision: A world where humanity thrives alongside nature, offering a blueprint for ecological and social renewal.

Braiding Sweetgrass: Indigenous Wisdom, Scientific Knowledge, and the Teachings of Plants by Robin Wall Kimmerer

Why Read It: While not strictly speculative, this book offers a vision of a future rooted in reciprocity, respect for the natural world, and the integration of Indigenous wisdom with modern science.
Vision: A world where humanity reclaims its role as stewards of the Earth, fostering balance and peace.

Utopia for Realists: How We Can Build the Ideal World by Rutger Bregman

Why Read It: A pragmatic yet optimistic exploration of policies like universal basic income and reduced workweeks, offering concrete ideas for creating a fairer and more peaceful society.
Vision: A society built on equality, justice, and shared prosperity, grounded in achievable solutions.

Closing Note

You are not alone. It may feel that way some days when the weight of what they're building seems unbearable, but I promise you, you're not. This world they're constructing, this cruel, calculated monument to greed and power, is designed to make you feel isolated, helpless, and small. It thrives on your silence, your fear, and the belief that you're fighting this battle on your own. But here's the truth they don't want you to realize women are experts at surviving cruelty. We have been surviving it for centuries, outlasting systems, regimes, and leaders who underestimated us at every turn. And we don't just survive, we adapt, we strategize, and we prepare. We learn how to endure, but more importantly, we learn how to resist. Together, we'll do more than survive. We'll outlast them, undermine them, and, eventually, we'll replace them.

When that day comes, and it will come, you can bet we'll do it with more style, compassion, and competence than they ever dreamed possible. That's what they fear most, isn't it? Not just that we'll take their power, but that we'll do it better than they ever could. We'll prove their systems weren't just unjust, they were inefficient, clunky, and archaic. Their greed blinds them to progress; their hatred blinds them to possibility. We'll rebuild in ways they can't fathom because their imaginations stop where their selfishness begins. And when they look at the world we've created, they'll see how irrelevant they've always been. Their cruelty won't define the future; it will be a footnote in the story of how we rose to something greater, something more beautiful than they could ever envision.

Until then, stay fierce. Fierce in your resistance, fierce in your love for yourself and the people around you. They want to break that love because they know it's what binds us together, and they know nothing terrifies them more than women united. That love, that fierce commitment to each other, is what will see us through. Don't let them chip away at it. Nurture your relationships, lean on your community, and, when it feels like too much, let others lean on you. We've always carried each other through the worst, and that's not going to change now. If anything, it's how we'll win. Love is our unbreakable thread, weaving us together into a force they can't control or divide.

Stay funny, too. Humor is your armor, your weapon, and your shield. Laugh at their ridiculousness, their hypocrisy, and their cartoonishly fragile egos. They want to be feared, to be taken seriously, to loom large in your mind like untouchable gods. But we know better. We see their flaws, their insecurities, and their endless, desperate need for validation. They demand reverence and respect, but we meet them with satire and scorn. Nothing strips power faster than laughter, so keep it sharp and keep it coming. Find your people, share your jokes, and remember that every time you laugh, you chip away at their control. Humor reminds us of our shared humanity and reduces their bluster to the absurdity it truly is.

And most importantly, keep your middle finger ready. For every time they try to silence you, to strip away your autonomy, to tell you that you don't belong, raise it high. Let it be a symbol of defiance, of resilience, of the fact that no matter how hard they try, they can't erase you. They can't erase us. We are here, and we are not going anywhere. Not until we've done what we came here to do: take back what's ours, build a future worthy of our daughters and sons, and ensure that no one has to endure the world they've tried to create. That middle finger is a promise that we will not comply, that we will not bow, and that we will not stop until we've won.

This fight won't be easy. Some days, it will feel impossible. The weight of it all might press down on you, making it hard to breathe, to think, to keep going. But on those days, look around you, at the women who have fought before you, who stand beside you now, and who will pick up the torch if you stumble. You are part of something bigger, something unbreakable, something they will never understand. This is the collective power they fear most: the interconnected strength of women who refuse to back down. Together, we are rewriting the rules and building something they can't destroy.

And that's why we'll win. Because while they're busy clinging to power, we're busy building something real, something that lasts. We're creating a world that values humanity, compassion, and justice. They fear us because they know the truth: we are the future. Our laughter, our defiance, and our refusal to give up are what will carry us through.

Stay fierce, stay funny, and never forget your power, keep that middle finger ready. We're in this together, and together, we're unstoppable.

Esme & Alice, Winter 2024

List of Prints

About EATMS Productions

What's happening to women now is not random. It's structural.

Policy, culture, technology, and power are moving in the same direction.

EATMS maps them clearly and shows how to respond.

This title is part of an ongoing body of work. All EATMS Productions titles, across all series, authors, and formats, are components of a single connected project.

Start here: EATMS System Primer — Free Bundle
https://eatms.gumroad.com/l/dyvzbw

For full catalog or inquiries: eatms.me

Free survival booklet + EATMS updates: email "EATMS" to eatms@pm.me

Please feel free to burn part or all of this book, safely, as an effigy.

www.ingramcontent.com/pod-product-compliance
Lightning Source LLC
LaVergne TN
LVHW050959080826
845145LV00009B/2357

* 9 7 8 1 9 6 6 0 1 4 0 6 5 *